Axis Stone Mysteries

LEG MAN

G. L. Keady

Published in Australia in 2023
by Big Island Productions

Big Island Productions
PO Box 3027, Tuross Head, 2537, NSW, Australia.
www.bigislandprod.net

ISBN:
E-book: 978-1-923038-11-0
Print: 978-1-923038-10-3

Edited by Canon Doyle
Cover design and art: Brandon Evans-Keady

TABLE OF CONTENTS

CHAPTER ONE

SOMETIMES BEING A private detective is as boring as watching grass grow, not that I can see any grass from my office window. But right now, I'm listening to the rain drumming an irritating, out-of-time beat on the window behind me. I like my sixth-floor office in downtown Sydney, or rather, Chinatown—the only affordable office space for a guy with the irregular income of a session musician, never knowing when the next paying gig will turn up.

I had been reminiscing about my last case and the beautiful Lovejoy twins. The fee had provided some financial relief, but I still needed to be frugal to survive. It had been a successful mission in the Philippines, but returning home to find my message bank empty was a downer. Beneath the stack of unpaid bills on my desk, my smartphone, sporting a new ringtone— "Someday Soon," one of my favourite songs— remained silent. I was willing it to ring when I heard the door of my unmanned reception open.

"Come in!" I yelled loudly enough for my voice to reach the front door. "My secretary is on holiday," I lied.

The office door slowly opened, and a Chinese woman, perhaps in her mid-twenties (though it was hard to tell with the COVID mask), poked her head in.

"Yes," I said, hoping she was a paying client.

She pushed the door wide open. Not a stunner, but she had sexy eyes, nice legs, bob-cut black hair, button-like breasts, and a good figure. She peeled off her mask but kept a safe distance. She was pretty, but she wore a sour look on her face, as if someone had just swiped her lunch money.

Her demeanour transformed to friendliness as soon as she fixed her eyes on me. My charming looks often had that effect on women.

"So sorry for the interruption," she apologised. "Are you Detective Stone?"

"You got it, miss... Axis Stone," I said, sliding my feet off my desk in an attempt to present a more professional image. "Sit down. How can I help you?"

She smiled, revealing nice teeth—demure, exotic. She wore no rings and dressed smart casual, just short of being designer gear, but still up-market hip. She was obviously well-off, enough to pique my interest anyway. I hate to be mercenary, but business is business. Just looking at her made my blood ferment and warmed the aircon quicker than a short circuit.

"My name is Jazz Sun... yes, I know, it's an odd name... my father was expecting a boy," she mused, with an angelic smile. "Mr. Stone, my father has a very big problem that is making him ill."

She looked like she was about to burst into tears, so I jumped up like every practicing gentleman should and snatched a tissue from the box on my desk.

"Here," I said, handing it to her. I sat on the edge of the desk with a concerned expression and my arms folded. "Why don't you tell me the problem?"

"My father owns the Golden Dragon Restaurant."

"Yeah, I know it... it's just around the corner. I've eaten there a few times—nice Gow Gees, good take-away."

"Thank you," she said, sniffing, and then elegantly crossed her legs. Her shapely bare legs and sandaled feet sent my head reeling—it had been a while. I was surprised that my gawking didn't seem to bother her.

"The restaurant business is very cut-throat, Mr. Stone, especially here in Chinatown."

"Call me Axis... Go on."

"Did you hear about the shark at Manly Beach last month?"

"No, I've been on a job in the Philippines. How does it concern you?"

"Well, two fishermen were off Long Reef when they hooked a fish, a big fish, a three-meter tiger shark. When they hauled it on board, it threw up chunks of the burly they'd been using to attract it."

"Lovely, I haven't had breakfast yet, so go easy on the gore, please."

"Well, it also threw up more than the burly, Mr. Stone. It threw up a leg... a human leg."

"So, the police went looking for a man with one leg?" I quipped.

"No, Mr. Stone. When my father saw the leg on the news, he recognised it."

"Wait a minute, let me get this straight. Your father recognised a human leg that had been in a shark's guts for goodness knows how long?"

"Yes, by the tattoo on the ankle."

"Oh, I get it. He recognised a tattoo on the leg?"

"Yes, the mark of the fourteen karat."

"You've lost me—the fourteen karat, you say?"

"A Triad gang from Hong Kong."

"Okay..." I mumbled, trying to get a handle on what she was talking about. "And that gang...?"

"My father's younger brother Chiang is a member, or was a member, not sure which."

"So...?" I prompted.

"He went missing after my father received a death threat."

"And why would someone threaten your father?"

"Because he won't sell them the restaurant."

I got up and paced the office floor, thinking out loud. "So, you think this leg thrown up by the shark belongs to Chiang, and someone carried out the threat by using him as burly?"

She began to sob, and I realised I had been too flippant when talking about the possible death of her uncle. I gently put my hand on her shoulder. "I'm sorry, I shouldn't be so insensitive. Forgive me."

She blew her nose and frowned. "That's all right, Mr. Stone. I understand your vernacular."

I moved back behind my desk and flopped into my '70s high-back swivel chair. It creaked and groaned in protest. Call me old-fashioned, but I loved it.

"So, what do you want from me, Miss Sun? You know the shark leg bit is a police matter."

"They are pursuing a different line of inquiry, Mr. Stone. They haven't made the connection with the Triads, and we have no desire to tell them."

"Why not?"

"Because the threat still stands, only now they have demonstrated their intent."

"Do you know the identity of the blackmailer?"

"No."

"Does your father?"

"I don't know," she answered sharply.

"Does your father know you have contacted me?"

"No, he doesn't."

"Then what do you expect of me?"

"I want you to find out if it was Chiang's leg, and if so, who killed him. Then, I want you to bring him to justice."

"I'm not an executioner, Miss Sun. I don't kill people. Look, if I were to guess, the blackmailer and the killers would probably be Chinese, am I right?"

"More than likely."

"Well, I have no experience in dealing with Chinese."

"Did you have experience dealing with Filipinos?"

"No, but I sure do now."

"I rest my case." She handed me an envelope.

I peeked inside at the three grand in crispy one-hundred-dollar bills.

"There will be an envelope with the same amount each week, and a bonus of ten thousand when you solve the case. Will that be sufficient?"

"It'll do nicely. If I take the case, how do you want me to proceed, given that I won't be killing anyone?"

"If you don't want the case, I will find someone who does," she returned with interest.

"All right... all right... I'll take it... so?"

"I will introduce you to my father as my lover. You will disclose your true job. If my father chooses to take you into his confidence once he knows you're a private eye, then so be it. But you won't disclose that I have retained your services. You realise that if the blackmailer were to learn you were retained, there could be further reprisals."

"Doesn't this put you at risk, Miss Sun?"

"Yes, but it's what is expected of me, though I must never divulge it."

"Cultural, huh? The daughter is dispensable but can act honourably on the side... is that it?"

"Family honour, Mr. Stone," she said, standing. "I will expect a weekly report from you and regular updates, kept confidential, of course. Here is my card. My apartment is nearby. Meet me at seven tonight at the Golden Dragon." A frosted gleam of impatience showed in her sapphire eyes for just a moment. Her demeanour had changed radically since she walked in the door—a dragon lady had replaced the gentle, demure damsel in distress. She held out her hand to shake.

"Thank you, Mr. Stone. I hope you're worth the money," she said slowly.

I leaned over the desk, took hold of her silky, pale, thin hand with perfectly manicured, long, red, lacquered fingernails, and locked eyes with her.

"I generally provide satisfaction, Miss Sun."

Her lips twisted in a bad imitation of a smile, and with a smug glare, she withdrew her hand. In the blink of an eye, she was gone, leaving me with a new case to solve. I pushed back in my chair, staring at the fat envelope on my desk, feeling pleased with myself. I checked my Mac—it was just after midday. Time for some research.

When I checked the time again, it was six-thirty. I would have to freshen up soon to meet Miss Sun and her father. My research of newspapers and a police database, for which I was fortunate enough to have the key, had yielded results. I now had a clear picture from the police perspective regarding the shark leg case. I needed to make the most of it and called my buddy and mentor, DI Malone, from homicide. He pulled up the case on his computer but had little to add. The case was growing cold, with no leads on the identity of the leg and few clues from forensics, apart from it being severed by a chainsaw. Without any fingerprints, it was a dead end, and the DNA had yielded nothing due to the limited size of the Genomic library. Malone asked what had sparked my interest in the case. Not wanting to lie, I told him that a client with a missing relative wanted me to make discreet inquiries. He suggested getting a DNA sample of the missing person, and he would check if it matched the severed leg. I thanked him for the lead and promised to return the favour if I found anything valuable.

For emergencies, I kept a brand-new white dress shirt, still in its plastic wrapper, in the bottom drawer of my desk, along with an electric shaver, a bottle of Davidoff Cool Water eau de toilette, a stick of L'Occitane aluminium-free underarm deodorant, a tub of VO5 styling wax, and a bottle of mouthwash—everything a guy needed to freshen up for a date. Just as I finished admiring my reflection in the wall mirror, I heard the outside door open.

"Someone there?" I bellowed.

A baritone voice instantly replied, "I'm looking for Axis Stone."

"You've found him. What can I do for you?"

He was a stocky Asian, built like a beach ball, making it easy to overlook his height. You could easily mistake his body for all blubber and not realise there was a layer of puppy fat covering powerful muscular tissues. He pulled a blackjack from his inside jacket pocket and slapped it into his palm.

"Sit down," he ordered.

I understood the demonstration and obliged by sitting in the nearest chair.

"Look, if this is about someone's daughter, I'm sorry. I won't do it again."

There was no sound, only a sudden, shattering pain as the blackjack bounced off the top of my skull, plunging me into a dizzying oblivion.

When the pounding pain inside my head had become vicious enough to force my eyes open, I found myself draped across the desk like a bundle of last week's laundry. Gripping the edge of the desk tightly with both hands, I slowly levered myself into an upright position and swivelled my head around, inch by inch. Fatso had disappeared but had left a calling card on the chair I had been sitting on. Unsteady on my feet, I felt the egg-sized lump on my head and picked up the card. It had the words "Sun Yee On" typewritten in English with Chinese symbols underneath. I rummaged through my desk and found some painkillers. I had never been hit by a blackjack before, and boy, did it leave behind a capital headache. It became obvious to me why Vincent Van Gogh had hacked off his ear—I reckon he had tinnitus, and it was driving him nuts. My left ear was ringing so loudly after the whack on the head that I felt like I had just come out of an AC/DC concert. I was running late—I pocketed the card, grabbed my jacket from the hook on the back of the door, and rushed out, headed for the Golden Dragon rendezvous.

CHAPTER TWO

I T DIDN'T MAKE it any easier having to run through the rain, dodging umbrellas like a rugby player. I arrived at the restaurant panting, wet, and with a 15K tinnitus tone still blasting in my left eardrum. A quick scan of the restaurant crowd failed to reveal Jazz. I spotted a sweet-faced Chinese girl behind the reception desk at the entrance, who gave me more than just a welcoming smile when I approached her.

"Good evening, sir," she said softly, her face framed by the black, lunatic fringe of her bob cut.

"Hi, I'm looking for Miss Jazz Sun."

"Ah, yes, you must be Mr. Stone," she punctuated with a sexy smile.

"What's your name, honey?"

"Rosy Tong."

"Tong and Stone?" I shook my head. "No, they just don't go together, do they? We'd never make a Vaudeville act."

She blushed. "Take the door on the left at the back of the room. Miss Sun is waiting for you there."

"Can I have it gift-wrapped?" I said briskly.

The corners of her delicate mouth twitched momentarily. "Stone and Tong?" she suggested sweetly.

I figured the desperate run in the rain and the knock on the head hadn't affected my sex appeal and fired her a wink with my best Mike Hammer ham-up.

I swaggered down to the rear of the restaurant and entered the private room. Chinese paintings adorned blood-red wallpaper, red and gold paper ball lanterns hung from above, and a single circular table was set with seating for six. Seated at the table was a stunning woman dressed in a black and floral-emblazoned cheongsam.

"So nice of you to come, Mr. Stone," she said in a contralto voice.

"I apologise for being a bit late, Miss Sun, but I had a visitor," I said, handing her the calling card I had been given.

Taking it, she casually motioned for me to sit beside her.

"And what did your visitor have to say?"

I took her hand and rubbed her fingers on the lump on my head.

"Nothing, he just left this relic along with the card and a permanent whistle in my left ear."

She retracted her hand as if it had been bitten.

"My goodness, why?" she said, trying hard to appear genuinely concerned.

"Maybe you can tell me? So, who or what is Sun Yee On? If I didn't know better, I'd think he was a relative of yours."

"Sun Yee On has nothing to do with my surname, Mr. Stone."

"Don't you think you better drop the 'mister' if you're going to introduce me to your father as your boyfriend?"

"Yes, Axis, correct." She put her hand on my knee, as if it was meant to show affection.

Just then, the door opened, and three Chinese men entered, all dressed in grey suits. The oldest of them approached, while the other two stayed by the door. I assumed the old guy was Mr. Sun, so I stood to receive him. He sat down without even acknowledging my existence. I remained standing.

"I assume you're Mr. Sun. My name is Axis Stone."

He motioned dismissively with his hand for me to sit and then spoke in Cantonese to Jazz. They carried on a discussion that sounded more like an argument. Eventually, they stopped.

I asked Jazz, "Is everything all right?"

"We were just discussing what to order."

She had me fooled; it seemed more like they were fighting over the bill. A nod from Mr. Sun and one of the henchmen slipped out and returned with two waiters. One topped up the glasses on the table with water, while the other took Mr. Sun's order, which sounded more like a demand. They both bowed and scraped, then backed out of the room as if he were royalty.

"Do you eat anything, Mr. Stone?" Sun said with a gruff tone.

"As long as it's cooked and smells good... I don't like stinking dried fish or offal. Tried some in Manila last month, and I'm still getting over it."

He chuckled silently to himself; I wasn't sure what to make of that.

"So, you two are going out together? Where did you meet, and what do you do for a living?"

"We met on the street, Father. We both live nearby, and Axis has an office in the Lee Kung Building," Jazz answered politely.

"I'm a licensed private investigator, Mr. Sun," I added.

"Does that mean you spy on cheating husbands or cheating wives?" Mr. Sun asked.

"Both, but I prefer to avoid that type of work. Mostly, it's detective work—finding missing persons, researching information, bodyguard work. Mostly, I catch the crooks the police have given up on. To better frame it, it's not what the police look for, it's what they miss that I uncover."

"Hmm, sounds like your motto. How long have you been doing this work?"

"I spent three years with an international private detective agency before branching out on my ace five years ago. I've stayed alive, so that means I'm good at what I do."

"Do you make plenty of money, Mr. Stone? My daughter is high maintenance, do you realise that?"

"I can't say it provides the regular income you would have from this place, but every now and then, I pick up a good enough fee."

The door opened, and three waiters dressed as chefs entered, carrying an array of dishes. The first waiter ladled soup from a large bowl into smaller ones and placed them in front of us.

"The specialty of the house, Mr. Stone... shark fin soup," Mr. Sun said.

I took a taste. "Hmm, puts a different spin on a man-eating shark," I joked.

He chuckled silently. "I like your sense of humor, Mr. Stone."

Again, he and Jazz engaged in a discussion in Cantonese, and this time it sounded even more ferocious. When a pregnant pause came, I spoke up.

"Nice soup. No leg in it, is there?" I said, eyeing Mr. Sun intently.

His facial expression turned dour. With a flick of his index finger, he dismissed Jazz. She fired a scowling glare at me before obediently leaving the room. Mr. Sun patted his lips gently with a napkin, looked at me, and growled, "Are you shagging my daughter, Mr. Stone?"

"Not yet, but I do have plans," I replied, devoid of arrogance.

Once again, he flicked his finger, and this time it summoned one of his goons, who glided over to us like a moth to a flame, drawing a blade and holding it at my throat.

"Whoa!" I protested and froze.

"I don't like white guys messing with my family," Sun snarled.

"Maybe that's something you should take up with your daughter. Now, get this goon off me, or I'll blow his family jewels off!"

The burly, skinheaded goon looked down at the .38 I had aimed at his crotch and tensed up. Old man Sun reclined in his chair with a smirk on his crabby face. He flicked a more agitated finger at the goon, who backed off and locked his switchblade.

"I could get to like you, Stone," Sun admitted.

"Get rid of the bookends with knives, and your chances will improve considerably," I said, slipping the firearm back into my leg holster.

He waved his hand, and the goons left the room. Once they were gone, he produced a pocket flask, unscrewed the top, and handed it to me.

"I'm not permitted to drink, so this has to stay our little secret."

I took a swig—it was top-shelf brandy.

"I might have a job for you, Mr. Stone."

I passed the flask back to him. "Let's dispense with the formalities... call me Axis."

He took a big sip from the flask, then let out a satisfied sigh. "Okay, Axis, you call me Ty."

As he discreetly hid the flask in his inside coat pocket, I studied him. He was in his mid to late fifties, regal-looking, tall for a Chinese man, with salt and pepper hair. His thin, pleasant face featured bushy grey eyebrows that shadowed a take-no-prisoners glint in his eyes. This was a guy who had survived the pool halls of life.

"I'd smoke if I were allowed to. It seems that when you get to my age, everything you once enjoyed becomes taboo."

"You mentioned a job?" I queried.

"It would have to be on the sly, with no mention of it to Jazz. If she hears about it, you won't get the full fee. Do I make myself clear?"

"Only if I take the gig... Go on."

"I assume you already know about the shark leg case; otherwise, you wouldn't have dropped that hint earlier. You were angling for the job, Axis, and I don't mind that—there's plenty of me in that sort of thinking. Jazz would have told you about my brother Chiang when she hired you. Yes, I didn't buy the boyfriend ruse. She doesn't have boyfriends, just handbags. I educated her well."

I was feeling uneasy in my chair. It felt like I had been set up, but the reason eluded me.

"Let me get this straight... you were onto our little charade and played along. Why?"

"Because it suits me, and we will keep the charade going if you agree to take the case. The reason for doing so will remain my own until I decide otherwise."

"Go on," I said, intrigued.

"How much is she paying you?"

"Three grand a week, and ten on completion."

"Okay, you'll keep getting that, and I'll double it."

Things were looking up. I liked this game.

"Before you say anything more, I got this calling card just before I got here, along with a sly knockout punch." I flicked him the card.

He didn't pick up the calling card. His eyes flashed on it, then back to me.

"That's what you're up against, Axis."

"Did he or they kill your brother and feed him to the sharks?" I asked.

"That's what I'm hiring you to find out. Chiang has been missing before."

"But Jazz said you recognised the tattoo..."

"That could have been tattooed on anyone's leg, just for my benefit."

"Why would someone go to that much trouble?"

"Because I've been told to sell out, and I won't."

"Is the buyer the number one suspect?" I speculated.

"I don't know who the buyer is," he shot back.

"Okay, so what do you want from me?"

"Exactly what Jazz wants."

"But why pay me all that money to do something you could have done through other channels?"

"Because if I make a move, any move, they will kidnap and kill Jazz. I know that. It is the way of the Triad."

"Look, Jazz said Chiang is a gang member of the 14K, and the calling card is from Sun Yee On, I assume an opposing Triad gang—in Hong Kong, mind you, not Sydney. I don't fancy getting caught up in some sort of Chinese gang war. I figure that's exactly why you want a white boy to do your probing."

"You've got it in one, Axis, and you will earn plenty of money if you succeed. You're right, this battle is being fought away from the homeland, but that's how it is with the expansion of China. I was born here; my father and mother immigrated in 1946. My brother Chiang went home to find his roots and found them all right—it brought us nothing but trouble. Yes, I suspect Sun Yee On is behind the takeover bid... and I admit I am dealing with an unfamiliar problem. That is why I need you, Axis. A Chinaman would not succeed; these people would get to his family and sway him, do you get it?"

"I do. I came upon similar cultural problems on my last case in the Philippines."

"I know. You came highly recommended by Nick Vargas in Manila."

"Nick! You should have told me that first up..."

"You know Asians don't work that way; everything needs to be a mystery."

I chuckled cynically. "Yeah, and don't I know it. It drives me bloody nuts!"

"Good, then do we have a deal, Axis?"

"Sure. Any mate of Nick's is a mate of mine."

"He told me you would say that. How will you proceed?"

"First, I'll need some hair belonging to Chiang. I assume he isn't bald."

"No, on the contrary, he has very long hair... a radical, you know."

"Yeah, I kind of expected that."

"What do you need the hair for?"

"DNA testing, to see if it matches the leg."

"Brilliant! See... already Nick's recommended PI shows great promise."

"Do you know the man who dreamed up the idea of subways was having a dump at the time?"

He liked my joke and laughed out loud.

"Nick also warned me to watch out for your crazy sense of humour!"

CHAPTER THREE

IT WAS GOOD to be out of the rain; one thing I noticed was that my ringing ear had finally ceased. I was glad that was over. I was tempted to phone Nick Vargas in Manila to get the dirt on Ty Sun, but decided to kick back, watch some TV, and chill instead. The meeting with Ty had been taxing. I hadn't spoken to Jazz again and considered ringing her, but settled on a rye on the rocks. With my glass in one hand, I removed my leg holster, stood up, and tucked my best mate, a Smith and Wesson Model 10, into the drawer of my bedside table. Then I strolled back into the living room to watch Friday night football. I was relishing my team, the South Sydney Rabbitohs, giving the Eastern Suburbs Roosters a thrashing when the intercom sounded.

It was Rosy Tong, the attractive receptionist from the Golden Dragon. I had given her my card on the way out, along with one of my more persuasive lines—that had clearly done the trick.

"Come on up, honey," I drawled into the handset.

I opened the door for her. "You look surprised, Axis," she said demurely.

"I guess I shouldn't be." She looked even better than she had at the restaurant—more mature.

She settled down in the nearest armchair and crossed her legs.

"Didn't you think I would come?" she inquired.

"Oh, I had my hopes. How about a drink?"

"I'll have whatever you're having."

"Bourbon," I informed her.

"Sure, I haven't tried that before."

"Well, there's a first time for everything, honey," I chuckled as I mixed the drinks. "It's the finest sour mash you'll ever taste."

She made a face. "It sounds like something out of a gutter."

I handed her the drink, and she sipped it tentatively at first, then finished the glass.

"I approve," she said thoughtfully, returning the empty glass to me. "I think more, please?"

After refilling her glass and giving it to her, I sat down in the opposite armchair to savour my own drink. "You know something?" I started slowly. "You fascinate me, Rosy."

"Is that so, Axis?" Her mouth twisted into a sardonic smile. "But I'm only a receptionist. What's the attraction?"

"You're very sexy."

"Seriously?"

She downed some more bourbon as if it were Sprite or something.

"Be careful. If you're not accustomed to that stuff, it can hit you like a mule."

She got up abruptly, carried her glass to the window, and stood gazing out with her back to me.

"Still raining?" I asked, turning off the television. My team had won, anyway.

She pivoted, tossed the empty glass into my lap, and peeled off her sweater.

"It's hot in here."

"Maybe I should turn myself down," I joked. She didn't get it. "Sit down, kick off your boots."

She moved towards me in a sort of free-swinging symphony, lifted the glass from my frozen hand, and drained it.

Her knee-length black boots made me think of a dominatrix. She seemed to read my mind.

"I hope I'm not embarrassing you, Axis," she said, looking at me seductively over the rim of the glass.

"No, no," I stammered, wondering what would come next.

With sultry eyes, she slowly sank onto the sofa beside me. Just then, "Someday Soon" blared from my smartphone — it should be renamed "Coitus Interruptus". I checked the caller ID. It was Jazz.

"Hey Jazz, no, it's not a good time right now … I'm in the middle of something. Okay," I said hurriedly. "The Grind Café on Sussex Street at 8 A.M. See you then, bye."

I put down the phone, anticipating some action.

"Let me take off those boots. I'm a bit of a leg-man with a foot fetish."

"Uh huh," she said, shaking her head and moving her legs out of reach. "I need to freshen up. Can I use the bathroom?"

"Sure, it's through the bedroom."

As she drifted off towards the bedroom, I relaxed, excited for what was to come. She stopped at the door and turned back.

"Axis, can I ask you something?"

"Sure babe, anything."

"Why did you have a meeting with Mr. Sun and his daughter?"

"Oh, just some business."

"Does she turn you on?"

"Who, Jazz? Can't say that she does … no."

"So, it's just business then? Are they going to hire you to find Mr. Chiang?"

"I can't discuss a case, honey, I'm sorry."

"Oh, I see."

She disappeared into the darkness. My excitement plummeted like the Titanic. I had no doubts she was going to leave; otherwise, she wouldn't have needed to freshen up.

~ ~ ~

Still nursing the disappointment of the missed opportunity with Rosy, I met Jazz for breakfast at the Grind Café. We sat comfortably, sipping our orange juice, almost like a seasoned married couple. She looked fresh and radiant, as if she was about to embark on a ten-kilometre jog once we finished.

"Well, I hope you got done whatever you needed to do last night," she said.

"Yes, sort of."

"We didn't get to speak after dinner at the restaurant."

"No, your dad cut you off pretty quickly. Is that normal?" I asked.

"Business to him is a man's world."

"You don't subscribe to that philosophy?"

"I think the world has evolved since the days when women were considered a sub-species. Which brings me to the point, did he retain your services?"

"He sure did."

"For the same reasons I retained you?"

"Yep."

"So, do I still have to pay you?"

"If you want to continue our contract, yes."

"But you've been retained by my father. Isn't that now a conflict of interest?"

"It's what you asked me to do, isn't it?"

"Yes, I guess you're right. It doesn't matter, it's all his money anyway. What is your next move then?"

"I need a few strands of Chiang's hair for DNA analysis, to see if it matches the shark leg."

She nodded. "I'll get his girlfriend to drop off a brush or something."

"Don't worry, I'll pick it up. I'd like to look over his place for clues anyway. Is that where he disappeared from?"

"Yes, she was at work … he was home. She found signs of a struggle, things broken."

"Okay, I suppose it's all been cleaned up since, so there'd be no point getting prints, but I still want to check it out."

"When?"

"As soon as possible."

"Okay, I'll arrange it," she said, typing a text on her phone. "I'll text you the address once it's set up. His place is a Darling Harbour apartment. There's something else I want you to do."

"Go on," I murmured.

"My father visits the Fortune Garden in Surry Hills quite often, and I think he might owe them money."

"Fortune Garden, isn't that a restaurant?"

"Yes, and a mah-jong room. It's the go-to place for wealthy Cantonese Chinese to gamble in town."

"Okay, so do you think they might be behind the kidnapping or the take-over offer for the Golden Dragon?"

"Maybe, I just know some of his secret habits, and Chinese men his age tend to gamble… sometimes to the extreme."

"Does he have a wife or a girlfriend or both?"

"My mother died when I was fifteen. I am an only child. My father has had many mistresses but I worry, Axis. In the last few years, he hasn't had one. Something else must be satisfying him, and it can't be work."

"All right, I'll look into it. Tell me, your father said he was recommended to me, and you told me you just heard about me. So, what's the truth?"

"Oh, a family friend recommended you. I'm sorry, I should have told you but I didn't know how my father would react to you."

"You weren't sure he'd hire a Gweilo?"

"Ah, you know the Chinese term for a white guy—Gweilo: green-eyed devil? We don't use it, we're Australians. But yes, I thought he might want to handle it himself… and I figured that'd be dangerous. He's too old for that sort of stuff."

"Is the family friend a Filipino named Nick Vargas by chance?"

She blushed, "Yes, Nick is a distant cousin."

Her cheeks flushed in a way that suggested a closer relationship with Nick. I examined her again. Yes, she was Nick's type—and mine as well, considering we both dated twin sisters Kitty and Lola Lovejoy.

Jazz had a similar figure to Kitty, and also his ex-fiancée, Bianca Gutierrez. Her skirt, riding up over her knees, offered a good view of her shapely legs. After the conversation with Rosy last night, I was beginning to change my mind about whether Jazz turned me on or not. Then I noticed her feet. She was wearing sandals that showed them off — they were exquisite, probably the best feet I've ever seen.

"Axis, you're staring at my feet."

I quickly returned my gaze to her face, as though I'd been caught red-handed.

"Sorry, I was just thinking."

"Thinking about what... a pedicure?"

"No, I was thinking that you have lovely legs and the most beautiful feet I've ever seen."

"Thank you, do you have a foot fetish?"

"Yep, bare feet and legs seriously do it for me."

"Well, we have something in common there." Our conversation was interrupted by the buzz of her phone. "Oh, I have to go," she stammered after checking the text. "I'll text you about Chiang's apartment. You can pick up the bill, considering you're on a good salary. Report to me as soon as you have something. Bye."

"What, no kiss on the cheek?" I complained. "I am, after all, supposed to be your boyfriend."

She rolled her eyes, turned, and walked away.

CHAPTER FOUR

I'D ONLY JUST entered my office when "Someday Soon", alerted me to a message. It was the address of Chiang's apartment from Jazz. There was no point in beating around the bush; I needed the hair follicles for DNA testing. So, I headed to Darling Harbour. It was only a short walk from the office, and the rain had stopped — the sun was shining. Sydney smelled fresh, and the walk was invigorating. The Shelly Street Apartments Plus complex, overlooking Darling Harbour and a stone's throw from the Barangaroo Casino, was one of the ritziest in Sydney. It would have cost Chiang an arm and a leg — pardon the pun.

I pressed the intercom for 905, the penthouse. A small female voice answered, "Yes?"

"Axis Stone. Miss Jazz Sun sent me."

A loud buzz signalled entry. I'd been in the block before. Expensive short-stay apartments occupied the first few floors, but the remainder were privately owned. A quick ride up in the elevator, and I was soon at the double doors of apartment 905. I was about to knock when the doors opened. I was immediately taken aback by who was there to greet me.

"Rosy, baby! Now, you, I didn't expect!" I exclaimed.

She looked irritated. The boots and outfit had gone; she was back to looking demure but grumpy.

"Mr. Stone," she said calmly, then permitted me to enter.

I scanned the room — it was a massive apartment, probably taking up half the floor. Ultra-modern in design and decor, with a chrome staircase winding creatively up to a mezzanine that likely housed a couple of bedrooms. Everything was white and chrome and designer, right out of Home Beautiful, except for several large, ghastly colorful paintings with a distinct Chinese flair on the walls. Rosy sat on the four-seater white leather lounge.

"Fancy pad... Are you just minding the fort or part of the furniture?"

"Chiang is my boyfriend," she snapped dispiritedly, and hurt.

"So, why the visit last night?"

"Because I'm left out of the loop. The Sun family treats me like trash. I wanted to know what's going on; you were my best bet."

I flopped into a big comfy white soft leather armchair opposite her. This time I could see her legs, but sadly not her feet, she was wearing ankle-high boots.

"So, here we are."

"In your official capacity," she snarled.

I surveyed the joint. "You don't seem to be doing too badly for a receptionist."

"It's an illusion, Axis. One puff, and it's all gone, just like Chiang."

"Is it a rubber glove or a gold digger thing with you and him?"

"A relationship of convenience for him, someone that wasn't going to give him trouble and wouldn't badger him about marriage because it was beneath her."

"A concubine?"

"You might say that, so no... definitely not love, just a better life for a girl from the western suburbs of Sydney, whose parents still refuse to speak English after being here for twenty-five years."

"Oh, my heart bleeds for you," I said sarcastically.

I got up. "Okay to take a look around?"

"Be my guest," she grumbled.

"The bedrooms upstairs?"

"Yes."

I made my way up the chrome staircase and entered the main bedroom. This guy was a playboy; he had all the toys — a huge round bed with a massive overhead circular mirror — the walls were all white, but the blood-red shag pile carpet spelled seduction. Any woman brought here knew what she was in for.

"You might like this," a small voice came from behind me, and Rosy pressed a button on the wall. Two chrome chains with black leather wristbands dropped out of a small hatch in the mirror above the bed.

"He liked to chain me up. Sometimes he'd go out with his friends and leave me hanging there... for days." She pressed another button, and a drawer slid silently open at the base of the bed. Laid out inside it like in a shop display, was an array of sex toys. Suddenly, the S&M black boots Rosy was wearing last night made complete sense.

"His choice of toys," she said, flippantly. "The ugly ones for inflicting pain were his favourites."

"You said 'were' in past tense. Sounds like he was a lovely guy, no wonder the shark threw him up."

I checked the bureau. "I'll need a photograph of Chiang. None on show, got one?"

"He avoids being photographed for some reason, probably paranoia."

"Yeah? Why's that?"

"I don't know, seems he always feels threatened or something. I've got one, I'll just get it."

While she went off to fetch it, I ventured into the walk-in wardrobe, which was almost bigger than my entire apartment.

"He's got more suits than the men's section of a department store, for Christ's sake."

Rose returned and followed me into the wardrobe.

"Here, that's him. The one on the left... taken earlier this year."

I took it and studied it. There were two guys and three attractive Asian women posing by a swimming pool. The two guys were archetype Chinese gangsters, donning dark wrap-around shades, dapper suits, and ties, while the three women were in the briefest of string bikinis.

"Who are the other guys?"

"No idea," she replied tersely.

"And the women?"

"Probably hookers, don't know any of them."

"How come you've got the photo?" I said, pocketing it.

"I found it just before he went missing. We had a huge fight over it," she growled.

I slid a large door open, "What about all these ties?"

There must have been a thousand of them, all different colours and patterns, all meticulously rolled up.

"No-one could ever get to wear this many. Does he wear them or just collect them?"

When I didn't get an answer, I turned around to find she had split.

After an hour of searching every nook and cranny for a clue, to no avail, I decided to make my way back downstairs. I found Rosy sitting on the lounge, sipping a drink. She pointed at a glass waiting for me on the coffee table. I picked it up, took a sip, and sat down.

"Hmm, nice drop, vintage Jack?"

"Yes, when Jazz said you were coming over, I ordered it in. It's Old Number Seven."

"You've got class, my dear," I said, taking a seat.

"Thanks for seeing me last night," she said.

"From what I've just witnessed upstairs, I feel a rank amateur."

"There's a world of difference between lovemaking and whatever Chiang calls it. All about himself and inflicting pain on others."

"So, if it was his leg the shark coughed up, then what happens to all this… and you for that matter?"

"All gone, me too," she said bitterly.

I downed the drink and then stood, ready to leave, "Well, thanks for the drink. I'd stay and throw a few more down, but I've got work to do. Oh," I pulled a hairbrush out of my pocket, "I'm taking this for DNA testing. I assume it's his brush and his hair?"

"Yes, it is. When will I see you again?"

"Let's just keep in touch, I'd like that." I turned to leave.

"Axis?" I turned back to her. She had slipped off her shoes so I could see her feet. She stood and lifted her skirt to give me a bird's eye view of her lovely legs and stunning bare feet.

"That's no way to send me away, you know that?"

"Well..."

~ ~ ~

I left the apartment with a glow on my face that could be read like a beacon from a mile away. I hopped a cab to the police HQ in Surry Hills. Detective Rick Malone was in his office at his computer when I knocked on the glass door. He gestured for me to enter.

"Detective Stone, sit down. What can I do for you?" He said, in his usual devil-may-care manner.

I handed him the brush. "Here, tidy yourself up, Rick, you're a mess." He was just about to brush his hair with it when I growled, "Stop ... It might be evidence."

He froze before it touched his mop of greying, medium length, unruly brown hair.

"Ah ha! The brush and hair belonging to your missing person."

"Exactly, delivered as promised."

"Oh, you're the height of efficiency, young man. I meant to ask how Manila was, nudge, nudge, wink, wink?"

"If you mean did I get laid, yes — was it good? Better than brilliant — should we go there for a holiday, absolutely, but your dear wife Judy might not agree."

"There's always some stick in the mud, isn't there? Oh well, so, you got what's-her-name back then?"

"Kitty Lovejoy?"

"Yeah, what a name — the mind boggles."

"What made it worse is she has a twin sister, Lola Lovejoy, an even better looker."

"Did you?"

"Client confidentiality doesn't permit me discussing that in detail but in short, yes."

"That's my boy! Now hang fire while I get this off to the lab."

He dialled his desk phone and mumbled into the receiver. A couple of seconds later a female uniform knocked and entered.

"Detective Sergeant Parker, this is my good friend, Axis Stone, he's a private investigator."

In her late twenties, her hard, sharp facial features were accentuated by her blonde hair tied neatly back, and her uniform.

"New, is she?" I asked, with a sarcastic smirk.

"Yes, it'll take her a few weeks to settle in. Either she'll sue for gender harassment or she'll fit in just fine."

"I think the latter might be the case, mate," I said with a smile.

"Now he's trying to crawl up my butt. Are all your friends like this, chief?" She growled.

"Yep, every single one of them," he smiled,

"Good, it's going to be great working here," she said, and held out a hand.

We shook hands and boy, did she have a strong grip. Rick handed her the hairbrush.

"Can you get this down to forensics, sergeant? We need it checked for a DNA match on the shark leg."

"Nice to meet you, Axis, I'll catch you round the traps," she said on the way out.

"Sure thing," I bellowed back, and then looked back at Rick with raised eyebrows. "Bit of a sort, eh?"

"Yeah, half the flying squad have been sniffing around her since she moved here from the south coast."

"No wonder, you rarely get a stunner like that working with you flatfoots."

"Ain't that so. Anyhow, you keep your filthy mitts off her, I don't want her soiled by your bad habits."

"How's Judy and the tin lids?"

"Kids! Cripes, tells you how long it's been since you were around for dinner. The tin lids have all grown up and left home. Judy's the same, plays golf, cooks wonderful meals and complains about my snoring — such is life. When are you going to settle down?"

"Not cut out for the happy nuclear family routine, mate. Besides, I've not yet met the right bird."

"So, to whom does the hair belong?"

"One Chiang Sun."

"Sun … sun … hmm, that name rings a bell. We got word on the shark leg case that there might be Triad involvement. The DNA forensics did determine the leg belonged to an Asian male."

"Well, there you go, we might just be onto something. You say you've heard of Sun before?"

"Yeah, something to do with a bust a few years back … now what was it? I know, an illegal mah-jong school run by Sun and other members of his family. He owns a restaurant—"

"The Golden Dragon in Dixon Street."

"That's the bloke. Glad the old memory is still ticking," he chuckled. "Vice shut down his little back room casino. He was only fined, no arrest."

"Speaking of that, have you heard of a local restaurant called Fortune Garden being a mah-jong school?"

"Only rumours … Want me to check with vice?"

"Why not?"

He picked up the phone, "I'll ask Bill Rogers … Bill, its Rick Malone, good thanks … listen, do you have anything on the Fortune Garden … ah ha, okay … thanks, I'll let you know if I hear anything. No, cards are on for tomorrow night, see you then, cheers." He put down the phone. "Yes, it's under surveillance for illegal gambling, does that help?"

"It's a real worry, that's what it is. How long for the DNA results?"

"Give it a couple of days. I'll call you."

I got up to leave. "Thanks, buddy."

"Watch your back, son. If the Triads are involved, it could get real ugly."

"I hear you."

CHAPTER FIVE

AS I WAS leaving Homicide, I realised by the pedestrian traffic that it was lunchtime. I was feeling a little peckish, but before I could do anything about it, "Someday Soon" sounded. I answered.

"Stone. Yes, Ty, I was just thinking about that. Sounds nice, okay, I'll be there in about fifteen minutes. Bye." I hailed a cab to the Cockle Bay public wharf in Darling Harbour where a Grainger Custom 50 Catamaran that Ty was waiting for me on was moored at the end of the jetty. I was seriously dubious about boarding it considering my abject distaste for anything that floats since my experience in the South China Sea a couple of months ago.

Ty's favourite two henchmen let me on board, and I found him in the galley seated at a table spread with steaming Chinese dishes. He wasn't alone; there was a man with his back to me.

"Ty, I hope this thing isn't going to move. I promised myself never to step on a boat again after a high-sea adventure that went wrong in the Philippines."

The man stood, turned, and faced me. "And what a great adventure it was, Axis," Nick Vargas said, beaming a huge smile. We embraced.

"Nick, you're a sight for sore eyes, mate," I said happily.

"Sit down, guys. Let's eat and talk," Ty said.

"What brings you to Sydney, Nick?"

"I'm on my way to meet Kitty in Brisbane. I was talking to Ty and he threatened there'd be trouble if I failed to drop in for a drink, so here I am. Have you spoken to the Lovejoys since you got back?"

"No, to be honest, I've been too busy," I lied. "And now I've got this gig, courtesy of your recommendation."

Nick explained, "I've known the Sun family all my life, happy to help in their hour of need. I went to Oxford with Chiang, you know, we played rugby together."

"A long history. Have you spoken to the police about Chiang?" Ty asked me.

"Yes, they confirmed the leg belonged to an Asian but that's about all they've got. I've given them some of Chiang's hair for DNA testing."

"Will they see if there's a match with the leg?" Nick asked.

"Yes, we should know in a couple of days. How's Dan?"

"Patched up and doing fine."

After lunch, Nick and I took a walk along the wharf.

"Nick, can I speak candidly?" I asked.

"Are you asking if what we talk about stays between us? If that's what you wish, Axis, yes."

"Okay, tell me what you know about Ty and Chiang."

"Look, there's a Starbucks over there. Let's sit and have a coffee," Nick suggested.

After getting a couple of coffees, we sat in the alfresco setting under an umbrella.

"Chiang is one wild and crazy dude. They're old money. It's rumoured old man Sun made a fortune out of the Japanese during World War II."

"Really?"

"Don't quote me, Axis. It's family mythos and not necessarily fact, but he did migrate to Australia in 1947 as a very rich man and was being hunted by the Communist Party."

"I was told Chiang is a Triad member. Is that true?"

"Well, that brings up another myth. Old man Sun was the head of the Sun Yee On in Canton, and fled with black money because he anticipated Chairman Mao would take power of China in 1949 and form the People's Republic, which he did."

"Either story puts Ty and his family in jeopardy."

"It sure does, especially when the old man and his wife were murdered here in 1959, then Ty's wife was run down in a hit and run in 2004."

"Were the perpetrators caught?"

"Ty has always maintained there are plants high up in the police force or in local government that shielded the killers, just as it happens in Manila. Remember our friend Mayor Rodriguez?"

"That reminds me, did you and Mayor Rodriguez have anything to do with the accidental deaths of murderers Ringo Raye and Arnel Gutierrez?"

He locked eyes with me. "Let's just say we had an agreement that came to fruition."

It was an admission that he and the sinister Mayor of Makati had conspired, as I had presumed, to have Raye and Gutierrez killed before they could get to trial. It killed two birds with one stone: kept the mayor's name out of the public record, and brought closure to the Lovejoy family. But it wasn't closure for the family of Ricky Esposo, my offsider, shot to death in a drive-by, or Chicki Dee, an innocent bystander who got her throat cut, leaving her six-year-old son with a decrepit old mother and no money. Nor for the Cortez family for the loss of Pablo, an undercover cop on a drug bust, murdered in cold blood by Arnel Gutierrez.

"With all I know, I can't reconcile that, Nick. I realise it's the Filipino way, but there's too much carnage to brush under the table, letting a crook like Rodriguez walk free."

"I admire your morality, Axis, but don't be under the illusion that this case is any different. Ty Sun is nearly broke. Chiang was dabbling in everything from the sex trade to drugs."

"What about the daughter, Jazz?"

"I think she's the only good thing about the family."

"Have you bonked her?"

"Yes, but a long, long time ago. I took her flower. But it was only that once when we were both too young for it to really mean anything."

"Can I trust her?"

"Yes, but always remember how thick blood runs with Chinese families. They're worse than Filipinos and much, much, more, crafty and... complicated. So complicated at times that even with my little bit of Chinese blood, I get lost in the chaos of their cultural hang-ups."

"Thought you have Spanish blood..." I said with a chuckle.

"Most Filipinos have a measure of Spanish, Chinese or even Arab blood running in their veins. Just watch your back, my friend. I won't be here to help, but I'll only be a phone call away."

"Thanks, buddy, and look, give the girls a kiss for me. Tell Lola when I get this one done, I'll pay her a visit."

I left Starbucks much wiser than I had arrived, thanks to Nick taking me into his confidence. But at the same time, I was left with a quandary: just who am I going to trust on this case? The answer was obvious — no-one. I headed back to my office to set my traps. On the way, I put my hand in my pocket and found the calling card from the Sun Yee On, and it suddenly dawned on me that I'd seen the Chinese logo on the card somewhere else: on Rosy Tong's ankle. That's why she was reluctant to take off the boots. She didn't want to expose a link to the Sun Yee On! The revelation only confused me further. I needed to sit in my office with a bottle of Jack and think it all through.

I looked at the bottle of Jack on my desk through the haze of confusion and thought: I'd rather have a bottle in front of me than a frontal lobotomy. Then, "Someday Soon" announced a caller.

"Jazz, hi, I'm at the office. Nick, yes, I know, I had lunch with him and your father. Yes, I got the hairbrush... it's with forensics... a couple of days they said. No, I'm going to Fortune Garden tonight for a snoop. Okay, I'll call you then. Bye."

I phoned Fortune Garden and reserved a table for 8 P.M., and then rang Rosy to see if she'd accompany me. There was no reply, so I left a message. It was an upmarket joint, so I decided to put on my best casual attire, expecting to hear back from Rosy before leaving — but I didn't. As a result, I headed off to Fortune Garden on my ace. I had thought of asking Jazz to be my date but reconsidered, thinking she might be too recognisable to the local Chinese high-rollers that I expected to find there.

~ ~ ~

A taxi dropped me at the entrance to what looked like a pagoda oddly positioned within a nest of residential terrace houses, typical of Surry Hills. Inside, the Chinese motif was even more spectacular. Had I not known better, I could have thought I had walked through a time warp and had been transported to Hong Kong.

A sweet Chinese lass dressed in a white cheongsam guided me to a table. She made me realise just how special both Rosy and Jazz were when it comes to Asian sensuality — this lass had precious little. There were few patrons, perhaps it was too early. I ordered a JD on the rocks from her, then rocked back in my chair to study the menu. It didn't take long before I noticed Chinese patrons being led to another room at the rear of the restaurant, which I figured had to be the casino. After ordering, I called over the maître d'.

"I was told I can play mahjong here?"

"I'm sorry sir, members only," he said stiffly. "Can I get you anything else, sir?"

"Just what do you think you've already got me when you ask me that? Pompous arse," I mumbled the last two words.

"I'm sorry, sir?"

"Just bring me another JD on the rocks," I ordered dismissively.

"Certainly, sir."

After eating, I fixed the bill and left. There was nothing to be gained from sitting in the restaurant watching the clientele when what I needed to see was the gaming rooms.

Later, outside Fortune Garden, I walked to the end of the block and found a lane that connected to a street behind the restaurant. My days of spying on cheating husbands and two-timing wives put me in good stead to find a way into the rear of the restaurant and, hopefully, the casino. In the street behind — sure enough — Bingo! Half a dozen wheelie bins marked FG were lined up right beside a narrow walkway that I knew would lead to the Fortune Garden kitchens.

Flanked by three-story buildings, the alleyway was dark but safe. No-one would be expecting me and if I got caught, I could simply declare I'd taken a wrong turn. As I closed in on the rear of the restaurant, I could hear music. The lane came to a fork. I deduced by the wheelie bin tracks on the ground that one way led to the kitchens — the other had to be to the casino. I followed my instincts and came upon a locked door. I put my ear up to it and heard music, voices, and glasses clinking. The casino, alright. Then, confirmation — I recognised the sound of mahjong dice being thrown on a table. There must be a window, I figured, so I walked to the end of the alleyway looking for one and found a six-foot wooden fence separating the restaurant from the building next door, and one floor up, a window — probably to a bathroom. If I climbed onto the fence, I'd be able to reach it. Rickety as it was, I balanced on top of the fence and then reached across to the window with my hand, hoping it was open. Jackpot — it opened and was just big enough for me to fit through.

I was right, it was a bathroom. The light was out — it was dark, but I could see there were three cubicles, three wash basins, and a mirror extending the length of the sidewall. With no urinals, it had to be the ladies' bathroom. As I started towards the door, I heard someone approaching from the other side and so ducked into the nearest cubicle and locked the door. The fluorescent lights flicked on and I could hear two women speaking in Cantonese. One of them entered the cubicle beside mine and kept talking while taking a pee. I was hoping the other woman wasn't going to get the urge to do the same. The door handle jiggled with her trying to open it and she babbled something that must have been a Chinese obscenity and went to the next cubicle. I was stuck between two peeing and chatting women with no idea what they were talking about. The first one finished, flushed, and then sounded like she was chopping up a couple of lines of cocaine on the toilet cistern. She called the other one in when she'd finished and they tooted up the rails. I thought no, now they're going to jabber on for the next half-hour off their faces, but they didn't. They giggled a bit and then left. It was time to make an exit before another encounter, so I quickly followed them out.

I didn't count on being the only Gweilo in the casino, so when I walked into the well-lit room, I stood out like a sore thumb. That meant it would soon be over for me, so I quickly scanned the gamblers not expecting to see a familiar face.

CHAPTER SIX

TWO LARGE BOUNCERS appeared out of nowhere, each taking one of my arms, ready to give me the bum's rush out of the joint.

"You're the last person I expected to see here, Nick!" I growled.

He and Ty came over to me.

"Old habits die hard, I know Axis, but instead of making a private eye entrance, especially through the Ladies, all you had to do was ask and we would have brought you along," Nick said calmly.

A quick word in Cantonese from Ty and the two goons released me.

"Jazz told you to check if I was gambling, didn't she?" Ty muttered confidentially.

"Yes," I acknowledged.

"She probably thinks I'm in debt for millions and that's the source of our problems, correct?"

"Something like that."

"Nick, am I in debt?"

"Not as far as I know, Ty."

Nick had already told me Ty was going broke, so he was covering for him.

"I thought you said you were going to Brisbane today?" I snapped at Nick.

He checked his wristwatch, "Sure am, the flight goes at twenty-three-thirty. Ty promised to get me to the airport on time. It's getting late," he said glancing at Ty.

"Come on let's go, we can talk in the car," Ty said, moving off with Nick and myself in tow.

~ ~ ~

We were in the chauffeur-driven stretch limousine just about to head to Sydney's domestic Air Terminal to drop off Nick when my phone buzzed. I checked and saw two texts from Rosy. I opened the most recent, which read, "905 help!" Knowing she wouldn't send a message like that if she wasn't in serious trouble, I tried to call her but only got her voicemail.

"What is it, Axis? Something wrong?" Nick asked, sensing my mood shift.

"It's a text from Rosy Tong asking for help."

"The floozy that hangs around Chiang like a bad smell?" Ty said dispassionately.

Ignoring his derision, I said, "I need to get out. I don't think she'd call me unless she was in real trouble."

"No way, I hired the limo. Where is she?" Nick said, showing genuine concern.

"Shelly Street Apartments Plus, Darling Harbour," I told the driver through the partially open partition.

"That's Chiang's apartment!" Ty exclaimed.

"Yes, where he lives with the floozy," I replied sarcastically. I knew he already knew this. "The very same floozy who works seven days a week for you as a receptionist in your restaurant."

"I don't know half of what goes on right under my nose," Ty grumbled. "I leave all that public relations crap to Jazz."

"You'll miss your flight," I said to Nick, ignoring Ty. His air of superiority over people rubbed me the wrong way.

"No matter, I can catch the 0600." He pulled out his phone. "I'd better call Kitty. She's supposed to pick me up at the airport."

After he got her voicemail and left a message, I asked, "Want me to ring Lola just to make sure?"

"No thanks, Kitty will get it. Besides, you might have some explaining to do if you call Lola," he said with a wry grin.

"I hear ya."

~ ~ ~

The Apartments Plus intercom was silent when we buzzed 905.

"How are we going to get in?" Ty asked.

I just smiled, and Nick added, "Don't forget you're with a private eye."

I buzzed apartment 902, and when a female voice answered, I adopted a professional tone. "Jenson Intercoms, madam. We've been having problems with the intercom and I need to check yours. Please press your entry button on the count of three."

As we made our way up to the ninth floor, Nick said, "Clever boy."

I wasn't so clever when it came to the sight that awaited us inside Rosy's apartment. She had been brutally murdered. I signalled to Nick and Ty to enter, warning them about the gruesome scene upstairs. They didn't handle it well either, and we all needed a stiff drink afterwards.

Ty argued about calling the police immediately. He didn't want the press involved and thought we should think it through. But it was a crime scene, and I had to call my contact, DI Malone. He's an old friend, and I trusted him to handle it discreetly.

I managed to convince Ty that we needed to cooperate with Malone, or risk him turning the case over to the press. After assuring him that Rick was a great cop, he reluctantly agreed to trust me on this. But when I suggested that this might be connected to his problems, he got defensive. Despite his doubts, Nick sided with me.

By the time Rick arrived, we had freshened our drinks. He was shocked by the gruesome murder, agreeing that the perpetrator meant business. After hearing the connection to Chiang Sun, Rick was convinced that we had a major problem on our hands. The notorious Chiang had been on the police's radar for a while, which only reinforced our fears.

As we left the crime scene, I asked Rick to keep the situation under wraps for the time being. It seemed to be turning into a Chinese gang war, and we didn't want to expose our involvement. Rick agreed, and we went downstairs to debrief.

After an hour of discussion, Rick called forensics to secure the crime scene. It was a professional hit and there was a good chance it had been cleaned of prints. In the silence that followed, I had a chilling thought. If they checked Rosy for signs of assault, they would find my DNA. Then, I'd have some serious explaining to do.

~ ~ ~

We took the limo to the Golden Dragon and retired to the private room to discuss our options. It was near 2 A.M. when Jazz burst into the room, all in a fluster like a woman possessed.

She all but screamed at us, "I just heard! Why didn't anyone call me!"

"Because it is a police matter, Jazz," I said.

"Come here, love. It's good to see you," Nick said, in his oh-so-cavalier manner.

They embraced warmly.

"I thought you were only going to be in town a few hours," she said enquiringly and then sat at the table, all calm and collected like a totally different person.

"So, did I, then this terrible thing happened..."

"But how?" she queried.

"I found them at Fortune Garden," I said with a wry grin.

"Ty was going to drop me at the airport for a flight to Brisbane. We stopped at Fortune Garden on the way for dinner and a little fun at the tables. As we were leaving, Axis got a distress call from Rosy," Nick explained.

"Why did she call you, Axis?" Jazz asked.

"I saw her at the apartment earlier, remember? I guess I was the only person she thought of calling when she needed help," I said, happy to gloss over the truth.

Before I could say another thing, the three of them cranked up in Cantonese. It came as a shock, Nick speaking it so fluently. I had him pegged to only speak Tagalog and English, but then again, he did admit to having Chinese blood. I guess that means the language comes with it.

The Cantonese was getting boring, and I was about to nod off when they suddenly realised they were being rude: by western standards.

"Pardon us speaking Cantonese, Axis. We are not intentionally keeping anything from you, just catching up on family stuff," Nick admitted apologetically.

I stood up. "Well, I don't know about you guys, but it's been a long day for me. I'm out of here. Good to see you, Nick. Say hi to the girls."

We shook hands.

"I'll give you a ring in a couple of days to see how you're getting on. If you need me for anything, don't hesitate to call," he assured.

"Thanks, mate," I said appreciatively. "We'll talk tomorrow, Jazz... Ty."

I left them chatting in their chosen language and set off to walk home. I was feeling out of sorts—the case was getting to me. I'm more comfortable when I'm in control, and this one was out of control. But the cool night air was clearing my head. I picked up the pace—my footsteps echoing off the cavernous city walls. I was alone in Sussex Street, and the full moon overhead had my shadow stretched out ahead of me like it was another person. I stopped. Maybe that's it? I questioned myself. What if it's all smoke and mirrors—shadows in the night? What if Ty really does owe a huge gambling debt? What if he used the deed of the Golden Dragon to secure it and now doesn't want to pay up? Why was Nick covering for him? I started walking again, but this time slower, more decisively. The cool night air had me puffing steam like a smoker. What if Chiang was doing a drug deal to pay off the debt and it went wrong? Have I been looking at it through the wrong lens? The first law of the sleuth is to establish motive, and the second is to determine the most likely suspect—I'd done neither. I resolved to get home and map it out on paper so I could decide what step to take next. A pair of headlights flashed from way down the far end of Sussex Street, which is one-way. By the time I got to my apartment block, it had reached me. It was a taxi, and it slowed down, hoping I was a customer. I pulled my keycard, swiped entry, and then passed through the double glass doors.

CHAPTER SEVEN

I'D BEEN AT it for an hour, mapping out the players I knew to be involved in the case and listing the different motives, but I was getting nowhere. What I needed was to speak to someone from Sun Yee On. I relaxed back on the couch. I don't know how many times I've woken up here on the sofa in the morning, still dressed, and I decided this wasn't going to be an exception. I'd only been asleep a couple of hours when I was jolted awake by the downstairs buzzer. I tried to focus on the time—it was six forty—and then the buzzer sounded again. I got up, groaning, and answered it.

"Yeah, who's there?"

"Jazz, sorry it's so early, but—"

"Come on up, if you must," I said tiredly, with a modicum of impatience.

I got the coffee on by the time she knocked on the door.

"Come in, it's open," I called from the kitchenette. "I'm just putting on a brew."

When I came out to the living room, I found her sitting on the lounge with her face in her hands.

"Are you alright?" I asked.

She lifted her head, and her big almond-shaped eyes stared at me. "Just tired," she groaned. "I dropped Nick at the airport and came here. There's just so much to discuss... it couldn't wait."

"It's kept me up as well, but the more I thought about it, the less I realised I knew," I admitted. "Why don't you just relax, and I'll get us that coffee. How do you take it?"

"Just black, thanks."

I went back to the kitchen, filled a couple of mugs, dosed mine up with a nip of JD, and then juggled them back into the living room.

"Here you go," I said, handing her a mug. It was then I noticed she had kicked off her shoes and was barefoot. She saw me looking.

"Sorry, but you did tell me to relax," she said huskily. "I remember what the sight of bare feet can do to you."

"Is that a threat or a promise?"

She smiled cheekily. "We're getting off track," she said, bringing the mug up to her red lips and sipping. "Hmm, nice coffee."

I sat opposite her in an armchair. "Look, you'd have to say it was the Sun Yee On who threatened me, killed Rosy Tong, and possibly your uncle. I don't think they go around killing people just to take over a property, so there must be more to it than that."

She held both hands around the mug, warming them. "Go on, you're making sense."

"Nick confirmed Ty hasn't got excessive gambling debts."

"How would Nick know that?" she questioned.

"You tell me, how close is he to the family?"

"He was close when we were young. He went to school in the UK with Chiang, and he visited us here during his summer vacation, but that's about it."

I raised a knowing eyebrow. "How long were you two an item?"

The look on her face tightened; she didn't like the question. "I don't see what that's got to do with anything."

"It's got to do with you being truthful. Someone in your family needs to be."

"Okay, we had sex. He deflowered me, but it was only the once, that one summer when I was sweet seventeen."

"Good."

"But of course, you already knew that."

"Yes, but I needed to hear it from you. So, would Nick know if Ty was in financial trouble?"

"Definitely not. Father is way too proud to admit that to someone as wealthy as Nick."

"Okay, then we can dismiss Nick's statement as speculation only."

"Agreed," she said.

"So, let's assume that happened. After all, you had your suspicions; otherwise, you wouldn't have sent me to Fortune Garden, knowing I wouldn't be able to get into the private club. Testing me, huh?"

"Sorry, it won't happen again. You've proved your worth. Yes, I've suspected it for some time. He goes there every day, for God's sake, sometimes for five or six hours!"

"Do you have access to his corporate and personal bank accounts?"

"No way! I'm female, remember."

"Is there an accountant?"

"Yes, Mr. Singh."

"Right," I scribbled his name down on a notepad. "Sing with an H?"

"Yes," she confirmed.

"Now, suppose Chiang was trying to hustle up money to save selling the Golden Goose?" I proposed.

She nodded. "Feasible. You thinking illicit deals, like drugs?"

"Yes, and prostitution."

"I wouldn't put anything past Chiang. You name it, he dabbled."

I stood up and began pacing about. "Okay, this is what I need— paperwork on the financial position of the family from the accountant."

"Mr. Singh?"

"Yes, can you do that?"

"I can try. He's not Chinese, he's Indian, and will be easier to talk to. What else?"

I thought for a moment. "I need the name of someone in the Sun Yee On."

"I don't think I can help you with that. I can ask around, but I'd have to be super discreet," she said with genuine foreboding.

"No, it's better you don't do that. I'll need to find another way."

She placed her mug on the coffee table, then came up onto her feet without hurrying. She crossed to me, standing so close that her body was almost touching mine. I could smell her citrus perfume.

"There's always a way," she said huskily, looking at me in a misty sort of way.

I felt my breath catch in my throat as she moved even closer until her soft, nubile body was pressing against mine.

"Anything is possible, Axis," she purred.

Just as things were looking good for me, "Someday Soon" broke the moment. It was Rick Malone; he needed me urgently at the station.

~ ~ ~

It was a cloudy morning, threatening to rain, but it didn't matter. I was sitting in the rear seat of the cab, totally on another planet, still savouring her citrus aroma. By the time I was sitting in front of Rick in his office, I had cast off my disappointment of missing out with Jazz.

"You look like something the cat dragged in," he quipped.

"Been a big night, not much sleep," I countered.

"I got you in because I want to discuss this with you before you go running off and get yourself into trouble," he said sternly, holding up a folder.

"I need a coffee before you lay this on me."

"White and three?" he asked.

"Better make it four. From memory, the coffee here sucks."

"You're right." He picked up the desk phone and pressed a button. "Two coffees, please. One white with four sugars and my usual, thanks, Sergeant."

A couple of minutes later, one of my least favourite female officers in the world brought in the coffees. I had nicknamed her Snap because she growled every time she saw me. Most people wouldn't even think of her as female; she was so hard-faced and testosterone-driven.

"Oh, if it isn't Mr Little head rules the big head," she snarled upon seeing me.

"Snap, good to see you're doing your job. I hope you got the sugar right," I said facetiously.

"I should have known it'd be you... four bloody sugars!"

"Thanks, Janice," Rick interjected to put an end to our verbal spat.

She put the coffees on Rick's desk, gave me the look of doom, and then bailed.

"What is it with you two anyway?" Rick pleaded.

"I don't know, just a mutual dislike, I guess," I muttered, taking a sip of the coffee. "So, the leg belonged to Chiang Sun. I guess you're not expecting to find the rest of him. Christ, this coffee's crook."

"It changes the priorities of this case, Axis."

"I was going to ask you about that..."

He picked up the phone and said, "Come in now, please, Sergeant."

I was still reading the forensic report when a tall, young, well-built, well-dressed Chinese guy entered and sat down next to me.

"Axis, this is Grant Lee."

"Hey, Grant," I said, taking his hand to shake.

"Grant is with the narc squad under Bill. He spent time undercover with the Sun Yee On, a Triad gang you're familiar with, Axis... I thought he could give you a heads-up because without getting to them, you'll be just pissing in the wind."

"You read my mind, Rick."

"Why don't you guys go down to the Royal Albert Pub and talk it through over?" he checked his watch. "I've got things to do, so I'll meet you there in, say, an hour and a half or so."

"Sounds good," I got up. "Catch you then, Rick," I said.

A quiet guy, Lee didn't strike me as being the kind to go undercover in a gang as barbarous as the Sun Yee On and survive it.

We walked to the pub and went inside. It was still early, and there weren't many patrons, so we had our pick of tables. We settled in a corner that offered enough privacy for our conversation.

"You take a drink, Grant?" I asked.

"Just a fresh orange juice, please," he replied.

I went to the bar and returned minutes later with his drink and a JD for myself.

"I know it's early, but it's been a big night. Cheers," I said, raising my glass.

"Rick already filled me in on your case, so I think it's best to tell you a little about what you're up against and how to deal with it," Grant began.

"I'm all ears, my friend," I replied, leaning in to listen.

CHAPTER EIGHT

AN HOUR LATER, I had downed two more JDs, and the pub had filled to the brim. Along with that, I was completely mind-blown by what Lee had told me. How he was still walking around in one piece had me totally mystified.

"So, even though they're only a small division here, they have serious muscle and fingers in every illicit pie you could imagine?" I summarized.

"Yes, plus they're intent on expanding and recruiting. I examined Rosy Tong in the morgue this morning. She was a member, but only a new recruit," Grant explained.

"How can you tell that?"

"The tattoo on her ankle was fresh. You get one immediately after initiation."

I liked the guy; he was as smart as a whip. I asked, "Then, do you think she was a plant?"

"Absolutely, an expendable one at that."

"What do you mean?"

"They butchered her because of you."

"What!" I erupted with disbelief.

"Look, they are all about demonstrating their power. That is what Triad lore is all about, a supreme form of stand-over, similar to the Mafia. They knew she was talking to you, they probably even commanded her to do so. Did you have sex with her?"

"Yes."

"Well, there you go. You're a Gweilo, man, very unlikely that she would do that... she wasn't a whore. She comes from a decent family. She did it with you because she had been ordered to... and then, her use-by-date had expired. Simple as that."

"Damn, these people are ruthless."

"Chinese women, especially if they're born here, do not risk their reputation by sleeping around, especially with a Gweilo. The higher her status, the less likely she would be doing it for enjoyment."

The bells were ringing—why did Jazz come from the airport to tease me? Why had it been so easy for me with Rosy? I felt used.

"Okay, I've learned yet another cultural lesson. Tell me this—"

I explained the situation with Nick Vargas and how I met him in Manila on the Kitty Lovejoy kidnap case. I also mentioned how he had deflowered Jazz.

"That's not uncommon... many Chinese girls are deflowered by relatives, especially in the upper class. As much as he is your friend, I think you will find that in this case, blood runs thicker than water. In the Philippines case, it was a Western girl, so your friend who had a relationship with the kidnapped victim needed you as an ally."

"Okay, I get the picture. So, what do you know about Chiang Sun?"

"Plenty. He had been trying very hard to break into the big-time drug trafficking business. He had a massage parlour in Haymarket... now, what was it called? Oh yes, Cum and Go."

We both laughed at the name.

"From there, he ran high-class Asian escorts, mostly to high-rolling Chinese customers from the nearby casinos. He would source the girls in China, fly them here, take their passport, pay them very little, work them to death under the guise of them paying off their debt to him—most of the time they would end up on heroin and staying on here illegally... that's what got him into the drug game. The girls needed drugs to keep going."

"And the Sun Yee On are the Chinese drug lords here?"

"Yes, you could say that," Lee said. "And Chiang needed to deal with them... but he was 14K."

"Ah, now you've struck a nerve."

"Old man Sun, the father of Ty and Chiang, was a drug lord in China."

"Yes, Nick told me the rumour is that he got out of China in 1946 with money he stole from the 14K."

"No, not the 14K... Sun Yee On!"

The haze cleared. It all made sense. This was a massive get square. Sun Yee On wants their money back.

"Okay, let me get this straight—Ty Sun gambles and runs up debts and uses the Golden Dragon as security. Brother Chiang is doing a big dope deal to try and cover the debt, but it goes wrong. The debt is called in, Ty has to hand over the Golden Dragon but won't... they torture and kill Chiang... but still, Ty won't give in. Am I on track?" I asked.

"I think you're on the money with that hypothesis, yes," Lee said.

"So, what needs to be done?"

"You need to establish whether Sun Yee On or Fortune Garden holds the debt, then figure out how to settle it, or they will go for Ty Sun's family next, and I tell you, it won't be pretty."

"He's only got a daughter... Jazz. How would they react if I was to front them?" I asked.

"Who, Sun Yee On?"

"Yes."

"They'd kill you."

I ran my fingers through my hair ruminatively. "Damn, what can I do then?"

"Firstly, let Rick deal with Sun Yee On. Secondly, find out the total debt and arrange for Ty Sun to pay it."

"What if he doesn't have it?"

He reclined in his chair and eyeballed me. "Then, he'll need to borrow it. Remember, he would never have mortgaged the Golden Dragon. Chinese don't like borrowing money from banks."

Just then, Rick turned up.

"Hey, boys. Can I get you both a drink?" he crowed.

"Grant's on orange juice, and I'll take a Jack on the rocks."

"I thought it was only Harvey Wallbangers for you?"

"Went off them in the Philippines. Too much tropical vegetation."

'Went troppo, huh?' He punctuated with his distinctive Malone chuckle and then headed for the bar.

~ ~ ~

I left for the office a while later with a contact in the Sun Yee On. I had traded with Rick and Grant for promising to stay out of the investigation into the murders of Chiang and Rosy. There were two sizable things on my plate to close this case anyway: one, to tell my clients that it was Chiang's leg the shark had thrown up, and the other, to find out how much Ty owed and arrange for the debt to be cleared. I would only use the Sun Yee On contact Lee had given me as a last resort. Besides, the contact was in Hong Kong.

Just as I stepped out of the elevator at the office, "Someday Soon" cranked up. I answered. "Stone, who... Nick! Sorry, mate, there's bad signal just here. Hang on." I moved away from the elevator to the window of the 6th-floor landing, just outside my office door. "You there, Nick? Ah, that's better. Can you hear me okay? Good... They do? Great, send them my love in return. I'm about to tell Ty and Jazz that it was Chiang's leg... yes, the DNA was a match. I'm sorry, mate. Look, I've just come from a meeting with the cops and a specialist in Chinese affairs... the consensus of opinion is that Ty is in serious financial trouble. I know you said that, but maybe Ty is too embarrassed to tell you the truth. Did you notice anything odd at Fortune Garden when you were there? There you go, if they would only accept your marker and not his... that's a sure sign. You do? Yes, if you could find that out, it would be very helpful. Okay, talk to you later. Ciao."

Nick had figured there was a chance his contact at Fortune Garden might be able to tell him the extent of Ty's debt. It was a start.

I entered the office but didn't like what I found—the place had been trashed. Someone had been looking for something and made a hell of a mess trying to find it. I figured I knew who had done it, but whatever they had been searching for had me puzzled. I rang Lee.

"Grant, it's Stone. I just got to my office, and it's been turned upside down. I don't know. You reckon! They'd do that just to frighten me off, huh? Don't you think finding Rosy gutted would've been enough? I'm glad you understand them, mate, because I sure as hell don't. No, don't bother reporting it... There was nothing for them to find... I've got nothing. No, they can't knock over my apartment... it's alarmed. Okay, later."

The next call was to Jazz to set up a meeting with Ty. I left a message to meet at 5 P.M. at the Golden Dragon. That was in two hours.

Grant Lee had put the wind up me a bit, so I decided to go home to check if the apartment hadn't been trashed as well.

Turned out it was fine. I had time to kill, so I decided to clean up the place; it was looking pretty grubby. As I was picking a glass up off the floor beside the sofa, I found an iPod sticking out from under it that certainly didn't belong to me. I sat in an armchair and booted it up. Not being up to speed on iPods, I opened a couple of apps. I wanted to know who it belonged to but didn't know how to find out. I opened settings—that didn't help. I couldn't read any of the social media files; they were in Chinese, which led me to suspect it belonged to Jazz. I opened the photo album, and the first photo was a selfie of Rosy. The iPod belonged to her. I flicked through the photos; there were over four hundred of them. The majority were of Chiang with other guys and dolls. I thought she said Chiang didn't like being photographed... and that she only had the one photo? To my PI photographic eye, most of the images seemed to be candid or spy shots. Then, I found one taken from the mezzanine of Chiang's apartment looking down. Chiang was in the process of handing over a large sum of cash for what looked like bags of cocaine, and the man handing him the drugs was none other than Sergeant Grant Lee! It dawned on me that this was probably what someone wanted badly enough to ransack my office. The important question was, did they want it bad enough to have tortured and murdered Rosy? I scratched my head, wondering if the photograph implicated Lee or if he had been undercover at the time. I double-clicked it to find the date. It was only three months ago. I was under the impression Lee's undercover work had finished by then—I needed to speak urgently with Malone. This whole thing was beginning to get ugly. I figured it would be wise to hide the iPod, go to the meeting with Jazz and Ty, dig a little deeper there, wait for Nick to come back to me, then speak with Malone about Grant Lee once he got home. I hid the iPod in my secret whippy behind the fridge. A shower and a change of clothes were in order.

Spruced up, I slipped on my trusty .38 and headed for the rendezvous at the Golden Dragon.

~ ~ ~

There were only a few customers in the restaurant at that hour, and there was a new girl at the reception. She had nothing on Rosy; in fact, the poor kid had buckteeth and could've eaten an apple through a tennis racket. She led me to the private room where I found Ty with the bookends guarding him. I stopped inside the door and waited for the goons to leave, eyeballing the one who had pulled the knife on me before in passing. I sat to the side of the table so my back wasn't facing the door—call me paranoid—but at this stage, I still had no idea who was trustworthy.

"Is Jazz on the way?" I asked Ty.

"I've been calling her... Did she respond to your text?"

"No."

"And she hasn't to mine. Should I be getting worried?" he asked.

"Not yet... Let's give her half an hour or so. Sometimes women get a kick out of being fashionably late," I proposed sarcastically.

"In the meantime, you obviously have news. There's no need to wait for Jazz," Ty said sternly. "What is it?"

I could tell he had prepared himself for bad news. I tried to be compassionate.

"I'm sorry to inform you the DNA was a match—the severed leg belonged to your brother."

He froze, the colour drained from his cheeks, and he fumbled his inside coat pocket for something. His trembling hand found a flask, and he raised the silver vessel to his mouth, draining it in a few gulps.

Just then, the door opened, and Jazz entered. We were both relieved to see her, and she looked wonderful. She was garbed in a classy brown knee-length skirt, a beige satin button-up blouse, and a salmon cashmere cardigan.

"Sorry to keep you gentlemen," she said, taking a seat. Immediately upon seeing her father's face, her outlook changed. "Is everything all right, father?"

"No. Stone has heard from homicide that the DNA of the shark leg matches Chiang."

It struck her like a left hook. She instantly burst into tears, moved quickly to her father, and embraced him. They carried on talking in hushed Chinese whispers for the next fifteen minutes, while I sat there like a piece of furniture.

Finally, Jazz turned to me and asked, "Are the police now involved?"

"Yes, it's officially a murder investigation. Look, I'm sorry for your loss, Jazz, but the stakes are getting higher on this case. When I got to my office this afternoon, it had been ransacked."

"Why? What would someone be looking for that you could have?" she questioned sharply.

"I've no idea," I lied. "The point is, we need to get things into perspective. Ty, I need to know the truth..."

"I don't know what—"

I cut him off. "If you don't tell me, the police will find out anyway, and all hell will break loose. Do you want that to happen?"

"No way!" Jazz snapped, then glared at her father. "Tell him, Dad."

CHAPTER NINE

I T WAS THE strangest confession I'd ever heard. I'd bet on the right horse all along—Ty was drowning in gambling debts. But there was more to it than that, much more. His father, Chiang Sun Sr., was the operations officer at the regional headquarters of the Sun Yee On in Canton, or Guangzhou as it's now known. It was a prestigious position within the Triad. That's where the family got its name, Sun... Chinese names are reversed—Ty's actual name is Sun Lin Ty.

The elder man fled China for Australia in 1947 to avoid persecution by Mao Zedong's People's Republic Movement. Because he had control of the treasury, he helped himself to a nest egg to set himself and his wife up in Sydney. Eventually, when the Dragon Head—the leader of the Sun Yee On—discovered the theft, he sent an Enforcer after Chiang Sr. to recover the loot. When the Enforcer confronted Chiang Sr. in Sydney, he claimed he'd taken the money to finance a branch of Sun Yee On there. The Enforcer accepted the excuse, returned to China, and relayed this to the Dragon Head. Consequently, Chiang Sr. became the Dragon Head of the Sydney chapter of Sun Yee On.

There was little activity in Australia to warrant a chapter back then. There was no room in the Aussie criminal underworld for Chinese, so the chapter basically fizzled out. By the time Ty and Chiang Jr. were old enough to take over in the early 1970s, the chapter had ceased to exist.

It wasn't until Lee Tai Lung, Dragon Head of Sun Yee On, was assassinated outside the Kowloon Shangri-La Hotel in 2009, that there was a regime change. By then, Sun Yee On controlled both the Hong Kong and Chinese-Canadian Film Industries—perfect vehicles for laundering income from illegal gambling, drug trafficking, human trafficking, murder, and prostitution.

In 2012, a new young Dragon Head of Sun Yee On was appointed in Hong Kong. Having been educated in Sydney, he decided to step up activities there and attempt to use the Australian Film industry similarly to Hong Kong and Canada, to launder their illicit money. When the Hong Kong Organised Crime and Triad Bureau caught wind of this, they informed their counterpart here, the Australian Federal Police. But it was too late—the delegation, including the Dragon Head, was already in Sydney in talks with Ty and Chiang.

This is when everything started to unravel, leading to the current problem. Ty and Chiang rejected the deal from the Dragon Head. Ty didn't want to be part of illegal activities—he wasn't willing to risk the honest and successful restaurant business he'd built with the Golden Dragon, nor his respectable community profile. The Dragon Head wasn't pleased; he believed the Sun family owed their success and social status to the money taken from the Sun Yee On reserves in 1947. He issued an ultimatum: repay the debt in cash or kind, or face serious consequences—which is what we're now experiencing.

In short, the demand was: work for us, pay up, or lose everything. I asked Ty how much they wanted, and he said, "Ten million dollars."

"What about the gambling debt?" I queried.

"That's just another brick in the wall," Jazz added lyrically.

"Okay, so I get all that, but why kill Chiang and Rosy?"

"They murdered Rosy because she had something on them," Ty said irritably.

"That's not all; she was a Tong," Jazz added.

"What's her last name got to do with it?" I queried.

"Tongs are a fraternity similar to Triads, but more like a Chinese social club. Nothing illicit—they're civic-minded," Jazz explained.

"So, was Rosy some sort of spy or something?"

"We believe so," Ty said stiffly.

I knew she had the Sun Yee On symbol tattooed on her ankle, which would contradict what they were maintaining, but I kept that to myself.

"They killed Chiang to force me to give in to their demands," Ty said bitterly.

I still wasn't satisfied. "Look, let me put my cards on the table here. I heard from a reliable source that Chiang was involved in a big drug deal. Surely, if that went wrong, it could cause his death and if Rosy was spying on the deal, maybe she knew too much."

"I'd check my sources if I were you, Stone!" The last word came out in a full-throated roar.

I rocked back in my chair with my eyes locked on his, considering his reaction. After a pause, I broke the silence. "You have only four options, Ty—pay up, join them, take them on, or let the police handle it."

"That seems to be the case," Jazz said morosely.

I stood up and said honestly, "I can't make a decision for you, but one needs to be made and it needs to be made quickly. You understand the urgency... Call me when you've made it. I can't do anything more right now. But there is one more question: was Chiang with the 14K?"

"That would have no bearing on our problem, thank you Mr. Stone," Ty said dismissively.

I wondered at what point being rude had become a substitute for charm with this guy. Just then, as if summoned by magic, two goons entered the room and stood on either side of the door with their arms folded like gargoyles, indicating the way out. Ty was trying to intimidate me, which I found strange given that I was supposed to be working for him. I attributed it to his mistrust of everyone. My stomach growled—I was expecting to get fed at the restaurant and was now hungry. So I walked up to the cinema complex on George Street and grabbed an Aussie burger from Hungry Jack's—call me old fashioned, but I need a slice of beetroot in my burger. Anything else is a fraud.

On the way to my office, I phoned Nick and filled him in on what I'd learned from Ty. It blew his mind. His contact at Fortune Garden had confirmed Ty was in hock for around two million. We agreed to talk later."

~ ~ ~

Cleaning up the mess in my office was a chore I wasn't looking forward to. I polished off the burger, brewed a coffee, rolled up the sleeves and got stuck into it. Turned out good therapy, I had a revelation: what if Grant Lee is related to Lee Tai Lung, the head of the Sun Yee On assassinated in Hong Kong in 2009. Ty mentioned the Dragon Head that took over had been educated in Sydney. It was another thing to run past Rick and it reminded me to ring him. With the place now spick and span, I sat back in my desk chair and phoned Rick at home. I told him we needed to speak off the record and he got the urgency. He agreed to come to my office, it would only take him twenty minutes. He liked a beer so I ducked up to the corner liquor store and picked up a cold six-pack. By the time I got back he was due in about a few minutes. The clock had just ticked over 10 P.M. when he knocked at the door. I let him in and handed him a beer. We sat down, toasted and took a swig of the brew.

'So, what dragged me away from the end of Monday night football?'

'Sorry mate, who was playing?'

'Oh, just the Dragons and the Sharks, don't go for either of them.'

'Huh, Dragons and Sharks ... sounds like this bloody case,' I chuckled. 'I had a confessional with Ty Sun and his daughter Jazz earlier tonight and learned heaps. I'll fill you in on it all but first I need a little off the record info from you.'

He cracked a grin. 'Ah, the old off the record bit.'

'I need to know when Grant Lee finished his undercover mission with Sun Yee On?'

'Off the top of my head I'd say mid last year. Why?'

'No reprisals?'

'No, he only did a report on them, no arrests were made.'

'I see,' I said suspiciously.

'What are you getting at?'

'Okay, here's the off the record bit … I found an iPod on the floor of my apartment that belonged to Rosy Tong, she must have dropped it there the night before she was murdered.'

'Stop there, mate, what was she doing in your apartment?'

'We were getting it on.'

He slapped his forehead, 'Holy-hell Axis! You know what that means don't you?'

'Yeah, yeah, it complicates things I know, but just bear with me a minute. Everything on the iPod was in Chinese, I couldn't read a thing, but I found a stack of photographs that were dated, and one of them taken only last month showed Chiang Sun handing over a wad of cash for three one kilo satchels of what you'd have to expect to be either ice or coke.'

'That's the sort of evidence we could do with,' Rick said cheerfully.

"Wait, there's more... the guy handing over the ice was Sergeant Grant Lee."

Well, didn't that throw a cat among the pigeons. Rick sat there glaring at me like a stunned mullet.

Finally, after what felt like ages, he ran his fingers through his hair and said with a sigh, "Okay, naturally I'll need the photograph. This isn't going to be easy, Axis, he's one of ours... but you did the right thing telling me, and I appreciate that. I'll meet with Bill first thing in the morning and come up with an MO, but you keep it close to your chest. You got me?"

"Good oh," I confirmed. "I don't envy your gig, Rick. There is one other observation, Lee Tai Lung, the Dragon Head of the Sun Yee On, was assassinated in Hong Kong in 2009. The replacement Dragon Head was educated in Sydney. You pronounce Chinese names in reverse, so Lee is actually the surname... the question is, could Grant Lee be a relative of Lee Tai Lung? What if he's the brother of the new Hong Kong Dragon Head? They're normally dynasties."

"Are you suggesting Grant Lee could be a plant by Sun Yee On to ensure the prosperity of their organisation here?"

"Absolutely, and that he might be a more important member than just a plant, he might be the Australian Dragon Head."

"Holy Mackerel!" Rick exclaimed, and downed the rest of his beer to ease the anguish.

I filled him in on as much of what Ty had told me as I could remember, along with Nick's confirmation of Ty's gambling debt. Rick told me to leave Fortune Garden to him, he'd have vice bust the place.

"Don't let that childish hero-complex of yours get the better of you son if anything breaks," Rick warned gruffly.

"Don't worry my friend, I'll work with you on this," I conceded.

It was nearly midnight by the time we'd finished talking, I walked him downstairs to his car and then I strolled home. Just as I entered the apartment "Someday Soon" sounded a message alert. It was Jazz, she wanted to speak urgently and invited me to her place. I sent her an okay and she replied immediately with the address: Apartment 1707, The Connaught in Liverpool Street. It was a trendy address only ten-minutes-walk from my place.

~ ~ ~

She was waiting at the door for me, dressed in a scarlet robe. I followed her gaze down to her bare feet.

"Oh, I should have thought to have worn slippers. Come on in, Axis," she purred, her sloe eyes watching my face like a hawk.

She flung the door open wide, and I stepped inside. I padded across the deep-pile carpet—it looked like a page out of Ladies Home Journal. The place reeked of luxury—clearly decorated by a professional. It felt more like the nest of a rock star than the home of a highly privileged Chinese woman in her mid-twenties. Jazz gestured for me to sit in an armchair opposite her on the three-seater lounge.

CHAPTER TEN

"**SORRY TO CALL** you so late, Axis, but I've only just returned from talking with Father at the restaurant. To say he's rattled would be an understatement," Jazz said with a sullen look.

"I'm sorry if that was my fault. I might have been insensitive considering the message I was there to deliver."

"No, it wasn't that... we were prepared for the worst with Chiang... it was the realisation of the four options you presented that floored him. That's what we've been arguing about since," she replied crisply.

I scanned the room. "So, um, what's a guy gotta do to get a drink around here?"

"Oh, sorry." She picked up a remote from the coffee table in front of her and pressed a button. A large abstract painting of a naked Chinese girl on the far wall slid to one side, revealing a cavity. A light flickered on inside it to reveal a well-stocked bar. "Help yourself," she said boastfully.

I cruised over to it, "Hmm, this is my kind of bar! What can I get you that you haven't already got?"

"Now, that's a leading question, Mr Stone. You'll find an unopened bottle of Jack Daniels Sinatra there you might like... I'll have one on the rocks with you."

"Sounds like fun, but I'd prefer a bed," I joked.

When I found the bottle, the label blew me away. It read: Jack Daniels Sinatra Century Limited Edition Tennessee Whiskey.

"You've got to be kidding. This is vintage stuff; it'd be worth at least five hundred bucks!"

"More like a thousand, sweetie. I said help yourself, didn't I?"

I cracked it, poured three-finger shots into two glasses, and added a little ice from a chrome bucket. Walking back to her, I savoured the aroma rising from the fine drop. She took her glass and we touched them.

"Cheers," I said, and then took a sip. "Ah, the nectar of the gods."

"Sit down, Axis. I called you over because Father and I came to a decision. I will be calling Nick in a while to ask him to go to Hong Kong to meet with the Dragon Head of Sun Yee On, and do a deal."

"Nick? Hong Kong? Why not do it here?"

"Because it is a matter of honour that can only be proposed to the supreme head... Nick has a good understanding of this, speaks the language, and he is family."

"Why doesn't Ty go?"

"We can't risk that. Which brings me to the second part..."

"There's more?"

"You will accompany Nick."

"Me! In case you haven't noticed, Jazz, I'm a Gweilo!"

"We have noticed, Axis, and that is exactly why you should accompany him. With you there, he'll be safer."

"But—"

"No buts, we're paying you, are we not?" she said flatly.

"Not enough if you're asking me to risk my life being Nick's bodyguard... That wasn't in the brief."

"Yes, I suppose you're right," she agreed icily.

"I've got my doubts about even getting paid what's coming to me. Need I remind you your father is in hock for two mill and change to Fortune Garden... and as he said himself, ten mill to Sun Yee On."

"I'll deposit forty thousand in your account tomorrow. Will that do?" she snapped huskily.

"Plus, a first-class open return ticket to Hong Kong and a Peninsula Hotel suite. You pick up the tab, so I can keep an eye on Nick, and you've got yourself a deal."

"Done."

I got up. "Mind if I get a top-up?" I continued in an even more casual tone.

"Help yourself," she purred offhandedly.

I went back to the bar, poured myself four fingers, and nixed the ice. The booze was too classy to taint it with frozen water. Like W.C. Fields quoted, "I don't drink water; you know what fish do in it?" When I turned around, she was standing up. She slowly undid the tie around her robe, and it fell open... she was wearing nothing underneath.

"Anything else you'd like, Axis?" she purred.

~ ~ ~

The next morning, I was in the kitchen of my apartment brewing a liquid breakfast when "Someday Soon" cranked up. It was Nick.

"Hey, Nick. How goes it?"

"Fine, Axis," he said. "What do you think of their plan?"

"I think it's crazy, but who am I to judge?"

"I hear you. I'm not exactly sold on it myself. If it wasn't for you going, I wouldn't even consider it," he snorted.

"So, you agreed then?" I probed casually.

"Yes, albeit reluctantly."

"When do you want to do it?"

"I was thinking of leaving today. Would that be alright with you?"

"Yep, I'm up for it. No time like the present, matey."

"Jazz said you want to stay at the Peninsula. That'd be my choice as well, so I'll tell her to make the bookings. There's a Cathay flight out of Brisbane this afternoon, so I'll get it. She'll get you on the first flight out of Sydney."

"Shouldn't we be flying together?"

"Not necessary. No one from Sun Yee On will know we're coming, so there's no danger. That'll come after we make first contact."

"How will we know who to contact?"

"I'll have all that. You just get yourself sorted, and I'll see you there. Text me your arrival time so I can have a limo collect you."

"Cool. See you tonight."

I'd just poured a cup of java, dosed it up with sugar and milk, and sat down to enjoy it when the phone rang again. This time it was Jazz.

"Hey, Jazz," I said easily.

"Hi, lover," she purred.

"Hmm, getting familiar, are we?" I jested.

"You'll need to be at the airport at midday. You're booked on Cathay flight one hundred, leaving at 1400 hrs. ETA 2155. I've copied Nick, so he can have you collected from the airport."

"Okay, I'll see you in a few days. Tell me something, I checked Wikipedia, and it says that well-to-do Chinese ladies only make love to Gweilo's for a reason... so what is yours?"

"Pleasure, Mr Stone?"

"Pleasure was mine too," I countered.

"Keep safe, Axis," she added warmly.

She was gone, and I was off on another adventure into the unknown, this time to Hong Kong with its Triads, Dragon Heads, and funny food — good grief. Since getting to know Nick and Winston Lovejoy my cases had been elevated from Nickle and dime stuff to high stakes, high roller: a unfamiliar place for a guy like me. I decided to ring Malone to give him my itinerary. He didn't think going to Hong Kong was a good idea, but then agreed it was my job to put myself in danger. He told me there had been a resolution to his meeting with Bill: Vice will bust Fortune Garden this week, and Police Internal Affairs will look into Grant Lee without his knowledge. I gave him the Sun Yee On contact Grant had given me, and he reciprocated with the name and contact number of the head of the Organised Crime and Triad Bureau, the OCTB, a division of the Hong Kong Police force.

~ ~ ~

Next, I found myself in a big, comfy first-class seat sipping champagne at 40,000 feet on Cathay Pacific flight one hundred, en route to Hong Kong. Eight hours of pampering and bliss followed — it made me feel like Lord Muck. The stewardess even produced a perfect Harvey Wallbanger. I was suitably impressed.

~ ~ ~

I cruised out of the arrivals section of Chek Lap Kok Airport in no time flat. First-class certainly has its advantages at the carousel. After passing immigration and customs, I spotted a small man in a white uniform, his hat bearing the name Peninsula, holding a digital board with a red LED light displaying "Mr A Stone." High-tech, I suppose, should be expected in this mecca of revolutionary computerised gadgetry.

He led me to a dark green Rolls Royce and opened the rear door for me. When I looked inside, I found Nick. He handed me an even more perfect Harvey Wallbanger.

"I think you might find this to your taste, Mr Stone," he said, raising his glass. "Welcome to Hong Kong — the Pearl of the Orient."

I took the glass and sank into the plush grey, kid leather upholstery.

"I thought the Pearl of the Orient was Manila?" I questioned.

"It's also Sri Lanka and Penang, but none so rightly deserves the crown as Hong Kong."

The half-hour trip to Kowloon was spectacular, even though it was night with misty drizzling rain. It was especially stunning when we crossed the Tsing Ma Bridge, then through the Tsing Sha tunnel, across a second bridge, Stonecutters, then into Kowloon. When we stepped out of the Roller onto the forecourt of the impressive colonial

Peninsula Hotel, the humidity hit me like a wet fish. I was instantly reminded of Manila's balmy nights. Though it was twenty-six degrees Celsius, the humidity was at one hundred percent, certainly enough to cause my armpits to leak like a busted faucet.

There was no check-in needed. Nick had everything under control. He led me to the Peninsula Tower elevator, which took us up to the 27th floor. We entered the grand deluxe harbour view suite, which put Jazz's plush apartment at The Connaught to shame.

I flopped into a comfy chair and took in the misty but still majestic view through the large windows of Victoria Harbour and Hong Kong Island.

"This must be costing a penny or two?" I grinned to Nick as a porter delivered my bag.

"Around two and a half grand US a day," he mumbled offhandedly as though it mattered not.

"Holy smoke, we'd better get the job over and done with quickly then!"

"Axis, we're here to do a deal worth well in the region of fifteen million dollars, so a few grand in expenses is chicken feed."

"Must feed the chicken that lays golden eggs," I joked.

We discussed the MO and agreed to be up early to start with a good breakfast.

~ ~ ~

The alarm woke me at 7 a.m. After shaving, showering, and dressing, I headed out to the living area where I found Nick reading the South China Morning Post.

"Good morning, mate," I said, taking in the remarkable view through the large floor-to-ceiling windows.

Nick lowered the tabloid. "Howdy, I've ordered coffee and croissants. Will that do you?"

I flopped into a chair opposite him. "Yeah, that'll be just fine."

"I got a text message earlier from Ty with a contact."

"Sun Yee On?"

"Yes, a guy who knows the way in... As you would imagine, it's not an easy organisation to get a meeting with, akin to getting an audience with a Mafia Don in New York, I expect."

"Yeah, tough... What's his name?" I queried.

"White Snake."

"What? That sounds a bit suspect."

"Apparently, he's a stuntman who does movie work, one of the best here actually... We already know about the Sun Yee On tie with the Hong Kong movie industry, so it makes sense that would be the way in the door."

"I guess so."

"I was warned only to ring him after 11 a.m."

"Makes sense. Movie types are generally night owls," I agreed. "Maybe we should pay the head of Organised Crime and the Triad Bureau a visit first?"

"The OCTB, I don't know about that... They're liable to put a tail on us which might ruin our chances of meeting the Dragon Head."

"True. Will my phone work here?"

"Yes, if you've got it on roaming."

"Cool."

CHAPTER ELEVEN

W E POLISHED OFF breakfast, then Nick, being a regular mall-rat, insisted on cruising the Harbour City Mall complex under Tsim Sha Tsui. After three hours of walking, I'd had my fill of Prada, Ralph Lauren, and every other designer label on Earth. The only thing keeping me occupied was bird-watching. I convinced Nick that I badly needed a coffee, so we returned to the Pen and found a table in the legendary Grande Dame of the Far East lobby.

You had to marvel at the majestic vaulted ceilings and ornate cornicing that swept you back in time to when it was built in 1928. Aside from enjoying unrivalled grandeur, I took in the femme fatale parade on display. The lobby was a magnet for the Hong Kong social set to strut their latest designer frocks. It also attracted its fair share of foreign tourists, some interesting, others best ignored.

I was busy exchanging alluring glances with a blonde Germanic-looking lass seated all alone nearby. She had the longest, beautifully tanned legs and platinum blonde hair, all wrapped up in a cute summer A-line cotton frock that rode up well above her knees. I was just fancying my chances when a nine-foot Viking, minus the horns, turned up and whisked her away.

Nick was on his phone talking to White Snake. He finished just as our coffees arrived.

"Whoa, he's an interesting character," Nick exclaimed, a little shook up.

"Yeah? Why's that?"

"He's been in so many Hong Kong action films. You don't really notice stunt men until you've met one. He'll be here in a minute; he's just up the road in Mong Kok."

"Do you think he's one of them?" I posed.

"I'd say so, but he won't admit it."

"How did Ty find him?"

"He said he met him with a Hong Kong film director when they ate at the Golden Dragon. They were in Sydney shooting an action film a couple of years ago. He told Ty if ever he needed anything done in Hong Kong, he'd sort it for him."

"Makes sense Ty would meet plenty of celebrities at the restaurant. It is, after all, one of the best Chinese feeds in Sydney."

I tasted the coffee and it was extraordinary. "This is the most amazing coffee I've ever tasted."

"I thought you'd be impressed," Nick said with a curt smile. "It's Civet coffee from Indonesia, rare and expensive."

"What makes it so different?"

"It undergoes fermentation inside a Civet, a creature a bit like a possum."

The word 'inside' prevented me from taking another sip.

"Can you expand on the 'inside' bit please?"

"The Civet consumes coffee cherries and then leaves the beans to be collected later from its faeces."

"Civet poo?"

"Yes, it emits enzymes during the digestion process that alters the taste of the coffee bean."

"Of course it bloody would!" I wiped my mouth with a napkin and, fighting back nausea, put down my cup.

Nick smiled. "If I hadn't told you about it you would have continued drinking, believing it was the best coffee you'd ever tasted."

"Mate, if you'd told me you were going to order it, I would have said no thanks."

"Ah, come on, drink it up. It's clean and a delicacy worth savouring... after all, it is forty US bucks a cup."

"Jesus!" I picked it up and continued sipping. "If you don't think about it and just relish it—"

"Yes, stunning isn't it?"

Just then, Nick's phone rang and, as he answered, a guy with white short-cropped hair appeared out of nowhere.

"No need to answer, Nick, I was just checking it was you," he growled.

Nick stood and I followed suit. We shook hands with the White Snake, a man of only 5'8", but with a hell of a presence.

"Sit down, Mark. Can I get you anything?" Nick asked.

He waved his hand 'no'.

"So, is it Mark or White Snake?" I questioned.

"Yeah, being a Gweilo martial arts master means I was given a Chinese name, so they gave me two. One that is known only by a few, and the more general name of White Snake."

"I detect a bit of an accent..."

"Yeah, born in Glasgow. Came out to Malaysia when I was twelve, lost both parents in a car accident there. Was adopted by a Chinese family, and until I was eighteen spoke no English. I started learning the discipline of White Crane from a master, then changed to Hung Gar under the kung fu master Ho Kam Wai Sifu. I moved to Hong Kong to train under master Lau Kar Leung, a famous stunt coordinator, and he got me into movies and bodyguard work. Rest is history."

He'd obviously told the story plenty of times before because it ran off his tongue like honey. There was no way either of us were expecting a fair-haired, hunk of pink-skinned Scotsman to be our entry point into the largest and most powerful Triad organisation on Earth.

"Can we talk here, Mark?" Nick asked.

"No, it would be best to go elsewhere or up to your room," he suggested.

Nick gave a nod to our waiter and then we headed up to our suite.

~ ~ ~

Mark was wearing a black sleeveless vest, black jeans, and red Converse runners. His muscular arms bore testament to years of gym work. The elevator was so crowded that I had to stand behind him. Being six feet tall, I was looking down on him and could see the edges of colourful tattoos that I reckoned covered his back, and I could also see masses of deep scars on his bare shoulders and lower neck. By the time we stopped at the 27th floor, we were the last in the elevator. Being nosy, I was curious about the scars.

We entered the room.

Mark scanned the locale. "I've been to this room a couple of times before, actors like to stay here."

We sat down and admired the view.

"What a view," I said.

"Yep, a pretty city," Mark agreed.

"Can I get you a drink?" I asked.

"Never touch the stuff. Tell me what you need? I owe Ty a favour," Mark said with a steely smile.

I'd seen his type before, friendly but cool, calm but with shark eyes — reminded me of the late Ringo Raye, my gangster nemesis on the last case in the Philippines. Only Mark had cobalt blue eyes instead of tawny. Certainly not a guy to be messed with, unlike Ringo, tough as goat's knees, I reckoned this guy could cut you down in a flash and not necessarily with a weapon, primarily with his fists.

"We need to contact the Dragon Head of Sun Yee On," Nick said tightly.

"Excuse me, Axis, but I need to say something to Nick that I cannot express in English," he said carefully.

I nodded okay and he spoke in fluent Cantonese. Nick replied. They kept it relatively brief.

Not wanting me to feel excluded, Nick explained, "He asked me if Ty was in trouble and I addressed the circumstances."

"It's okay, I understand, so can you help?" I asked.

"It will take a couple of days but I'll do my best, no guarantees. If you have a contact in the OCTB, I hope you haven't told him you're here," he warned.

"No, but I do have a contact. I would only use it if all else fails," I admitted a little sheepishly.

"You are a sensible private eye, Stone. I've worked with a couple from the States, do you know Danny Green?"

"From San Francisco, I've certainly heard of him but never had the pleasure," I confirmed.

"If you don't mind me asking, how did you get the scars on your back?" I enquired tentatively.

He stopped, waited a couple of beats, then eyeballed me.

"I got chopped up by a gang of Triads with meat cleavers and was left to bleed out in an alleyway. Why? Because they didn't like me — it was twelve years ago. By the time I dragged myself up the alley to a main street and finally got to hospital, I had one fluid ounce of blood left in my entire body — according to the quacks I should've been dead meat."

The naked savagery in his voice sent a chill up and down my spine.

"Satisfied?" he said.

I don't think he blinked once through the entire spiel.

"I'll meet you at the Four Fingers Club in Mong Kok, at midnight tonight. There's a card game in the back room, you won't be asked to play. There will probably be powerful Triads at the table … they will be watching to determine if you are copacetic. Do I make myself clear? You will be tested."

He eyeballed us one at a time, the chill had made it down to the soles of my feet. I just nodded with my mouth open. I'd met plenty of tough guys before but when it comes to heavy with a capital H, this bloke takes the cake.

Nick walked him to the door and let him out. When he returned, he flopped into a chair and let out a long sigh.

"Phew, that guy was heavy duty."

"Better get used to it, mate. I think things are about to get even heavier," I said gravely.

By the look on Nick's face, I don't think he was too thrilled by the thought.

~ ~ ~

We spent the rest of the day sightseeing on the Island, and then headed back to Kowloon side for dinner at one of Nick's favourite restaurants: Jimmy's Kitchen. He had promised there would be no nasty surprises on the menu, and he was right, it was probably the best ribeye steak I'd ever eaten. The maître d' knew Nick, so we were treated like royalty. We polished off a couple of bottles of fine red, and by the time we left, it was with wobbly knees.

Kowloon was alive with people that night, and it took us a while to catch a cab. Nick had found the address of the Four Fingers Club, so he knew it was near the famous Temple Street night markets. We finally caught a cab and within twenty minutes we were dropped off at Temple Street.

Part of the street was closed off at night for the market, which, because it was near midnight, was in the process of closing down. We walked down Saigon Street to the corner of Battery Street and looked for the club. Thankfully, I was with Nick because the sign for the club was in Chinese; it was the only neon in that section of the otherwise dark and ominous backstreet.

"It feels creepy here," Nick said.

After the adventures we'd been through together in the Philippines, I knew that if Nick said that, he sensed danger. I felt it as well. I've walked the cobblestones of many eerie red-light district alleys in my time, and this one had all the hallmarks of the underworld.

"You're not alone, mate. You could cut the air with a knife," I agreed.

Nick opened the door to the club and I followed him inside. It was then that I sorely missed my trusty .38 companion.

The place was a rogue's gallery, with each of the twenty or so patrons seated at the ten tables in the dimly lit room immediately turning to look at us as we entered. Streams of smoke drifted through the room and a guy standing under a single spotlight on a tiny stage was butchering "My Way" — I can't stand karaoke. I've never understood why people pay money to sit around and listen to mostly untalented, half-drunk, over-fifty executive businessmen sing out of tune. I'd rather watch a tumble dryer; at least it stays in tune.

We ignored the lack of applause and made our way down the six or so stairs into the basement-type club. Nick nodded at two burly goons standing on either side of a door at the back of the room. A bar extended the length of the side-wall, with a few people seated at it on stools. It seemed out of balance, mostly men, only two or three women in the entire room.

I followed Nick to the back of the room. He spoke to the goons in Chinese. All I recognized in the exchange was the name "White Snake." They let us through the door. The musty, smelly corridor was like we were headed for the restrooms. We came upon another door, this one with an old-fashioned speakeasy peephole and a knocker. Nick knocked. The viewer opened and a tawny eye gazed at us from the other side of the door.

"This is a trip into the past, I feel like Mickey Spillane," I mumbled.

Nick chuckled. The latch clunked, the door creaked open, and we were ushered inside by a stunning-looking Chinese woman dressed in a red cheongsam that clung to her shapely body like cling wrap. Things were certainly beginning to look up.

CHAPTER TWELVE

THE GAMBLING ROOM was a stark contrast to the rest of the club. It was elegant and tastefully decorated, exhibiting a Chinese aesthetic with copious amounts of red and gold. The centrepiece was a large round table where a dozen men were engrossed in a game of cards, their faces lit by the light overhead and obscured by the haze of cigar smoke. Health regulations clearly didn't apply here. Mark, the White Snake, was one of the players. On noticing us, he stood up and approached.

"Glad you could make it fellers ... I won't make any introductions, that's not done. Do you want to sit in and play or sit at the bar?" He gestured towards the bar that ran along the side wall. "Or you're welcome to sit at a table over there and have Suzie serve you."

He was referring to several smaller tables set away from the card game.

"We won't play, we'll just take a table and enjoy Suzie's service," I responded, maintaining an easy demeanour.

Mark returned to his game while we settled at one of the smaller tables. Suzie, a vision of grace, floated over to us with menus. It was all Chinese to me but Nick seemed to understand.

"You hungry or thirsty?" he asked.

My eyes followed Suzie as she moved away. "I'll just take a JD on ice."

"No Wallbanger?"

"Not prepared to take the risk, this looks like a high-vegetation joint," I chuckled.

Suzie had caught my order and Nick added his. "Tea for me, please."

As Suzie sashayed off to fetch our orders, I leaned over to Nick and asked in a hushed voice, "You think she'd be available for a date?"

"Who, the waitress? No, I don't think so. You'd have to go to the Gweilo bars in Wan Chai if you want to chase fluff."

The background music was a soft, soothing pipa melody, and the occasional muted conversation from the poker players gave the atmosphere a library-like hush. Suzie returned with my bourbon and a pot of jasmine tea for Nick.

While she was pouring the tea, I ventured, "Can I buy you a drink Suzie?"

"No thank you, sir," she replied, her face settling into a guarded expression. She took off before I could say anything else, looking like she expected me to latch my teeth into her.

Nick burst out laughing. "Axis, you kill me. There's never a dull moment around you."

"My motto is you only get what you ask for."

"Makes a lot of sense. I like it. Mind if I use it?" he asked, chuckling.

"Yeah, what is it with you Asians? Can't you invent anything of your own?"

"No, we can only copy," he laughed. "But we do a better job at that than you Gweilos."

~ ~ ~

After sitting for three hours, with me downing four JD's and Nick on his second pot of tea, Mark sauntered over.

"The game is just about finished. Come again, same time tomorrow night, you might find it more productive," he suggested.

Nick stood and I followed suit, though I was feeling a bit miffed. "Thank you, Mark," Nick said, maintaining his grace.

As Suzie arrived with the bill, which Nick promptly paid in cash, I seized the moment to invite her for lunch. "Have lunch with me at the Peninsula, today?" Her eyes flashed at me like a warning. Undeterred, I whispered, "Meet me at 1 P.M, in the lobby, I'll be waiting for you."

She didn't acknowledge my invitation, simply opening the door for us to exit.

There were no cabs nearby, so we walked all the way to Jordan Road before successfully hailing one. We reached our hotel room about an hour later. With little to discuss due to the lack of activity, we decided to call it a night.

~ ~ ~

The next morning started with "Someday Soon", it was Jazz, eager for an update. There wasn't much to tell her but she was impressed by our meeting with the White Snake and that we'd been invited to the Four Fingers Club. She seemed to have a better understanding of the proceedings than I did, explaining that the Sun Yee On had invited us just to see what we looked like and how we reacted to being ignored. She predicted that our next visit would result in us making contact.

Nick had a lunch meeting at the Royal Hong Kong Yacht Club with an old friend. I took down the address, assuring him that I'd meet him there, as I was hopeful that Suzie would accept my lunch invitation.

~ ~ ~

It was one fifteen and Suzie hadn't shown. I was about to call it quits when an exotic beauty dressed in a beige trench coat and dark glasses glided into the lobby — I instinctively knew it was her. I approached her.

"Suzie, good to see you. Just for a moment there, I thought you were going to stand me up," I said, my tone warm.

"Take me to your room," she demanded, like a character straight out of a James Bond film.

I bought into the espionage trip and guided her to my room.

Once inside, she promptly shed her coat and sunglasses before taking a seat on a lounge chair.

"Why all the spy stuff?" I asked, my voice calm as I took a seat across from her.

She crossed her slender, bare legs. "I work for very dangerous people," she confessed in heavily accented English.

"So, you don't have much freedom?"

"Let's just say it is heavily restricted. What do I call you?" she inquired softly.

"Axis."

"And what do you do, Axis?"

"I'm a private detective."

"Hmm, how exciting."

"It has its moments."

I took my time studying her; the delicate beauty of her oval face, high cheekbones, the slender grace of her body, the small twin peaks of her chest, the softly rounded curve of her hips.

"What do you want from me, Axis?" she cheekily asked, her red lips forming a perfect pout.

"I want so much it hurts," I confessed.

"And then?"

"You want me. I want you. What could be simpler than that?"

Alas, all good things must come to an end. At 3 P.M., she disappeared into the bustling streets of Hong Kong, leaving behind only her intoxicating fragrance and a cherished memory.

~ ~ ~

I sauntered into the Royal Hong Kong Yacht Club and approached the reception desk. The girl behind it was striking, and I could see a spark of interest in her eyes. As she went to fetch Nick, I couldn't help but feel fortunate that Asian women found me appealing. This newfound attraction opened up an entirely new world of possibilities for me. After all, there was a wealth of Chinese women to choose from.

Nick emerged from a corridor and gestured for me to follow him into the bar where his friend was waiting.

"Ian, meet Axis Stone, the chap I was telling you about," Nick introduced me, his tone mirroring the nautical surroundings.

Ian was a burly yachtsman with a Canadian accent. After exchanging firm handshakes, we settled into our seats.

"Nick was telling me about your little South China Sea adventure," Ian chuckled.

"I assume he also told you that it resulted in a life-long maritime allergy for me? And, for the record, it wasn't a 'little adventure'," I corrected him. We all shared a laugh.

"What can I get you, sportsman?" Ian asked.

"A Harvey Wallbanger, hold the vegetation," I responded with a smirk, curious to see if the RHKYC could meet my expectations.

Ian ordered the drink and when it arrived, I was pleasantly surprised.

"A bit more refined than the Manila Yacht Club, wouldn't you agree, Axis?" Nick asked with a smug smile, referring to the drink.

"Absolutely," I replied approvingly. "Cheers!"

Ian turned out to be not only the Commodore of the RHKYC but also a lawyer. He'd participated in every South China Sea yacht race since the late 80s and had a repertoire of seafaring tales that would put Herman Melville to shame. But it was his insights into the Sun Yee On and the 14K that intrigued me most.

"Ever since the handover in 1995, there's been a street war in Hong Kong between the rival gangs," he explained.

"Haven't they always been adversaries?" Nick asked.

"Indeed, but not here. This was predominantly the 14K's territory, but that all changed after the handover. They're basically battling for control of the underworld. Hong Kong has always been a place of law and order — the cops representing the law, and 14K maintaining order. There was an unspoken agreement pre-handover. The Brits knew how to manage that from their experiences in Northern Ireland and India. But when they left, so did the alliance. The Sun Yee On migrated from the mainland and quickly took over the lucrative Hong Kong film industry."

"So, the fight continues then. Which gang is stronger?" I asked.

"That's debatable. The 14K has the numbers, but the Sun Yee On wield more influence," Ian elaborated.

"And which has infiltrated the police?" Nick pressed.

"That's a question that could land you in hot water, but I'd wager it's the Sun Yee On."

"Are they expanding into other countries?" I asked.

"Just follow the Hong Kong film industry to find out. They've reached Canada, Hollywood, and now, as I understand it, they're making inroads into Australia."

"That's consistent with our findings," I confirmed.

"Look, you have to be very careful sticking your noses into Triad business here, you just never know who you're talking to and these people are ruthless. Only last year an extremely wealthy friend of mine was found in Hong Kong harbour with a bullet hole in the back of his skull. Seems he had been bonking a Triad's girl. Even with all his money, he couldn't buy them off — first he knew of the threat was when he was crossing Nathan Road at the lights in the middle of a workday. A guy came up behind him and stabbed a long thin razor-sharp stiletto blade through his pants into his butt-hole, slashed it from side to side lacerating it big time and then moved off without my friend ever seeing him. He couldn't sit down for weeks, couldn't crap without excruciating pain but he kept right on bonking his concubine and next minute they were dragging him out of Hong Kong harbour."

The thought of Suzie being involved with a Triad sent a chill down my spine.

"That tactic is also used in Kuala Lumpur. Assassins often hide the blade in a folded newspaper," Nick chimed in.

"Yes, the job is usually part of an initiation for young Triad recruits," Ian added.

"Just a quick stab and a couple of swift slashes, and you're done for," Nick finished, flashing a dark grin.

The mere thought made me wince.

CHAPTER THIRTEEN

NICK WANTED TO take the Star Ferry back across from Hong Kong Island to Tsim Sha Tsui, but when I reminded him of my aversion to all things maritime, he agreed for us to take the MTR.

We boarded the train at Tiu Keng Leng Station. Being rush hour, it was packed to the rafters. Squeezed in the carriage like a sardine, I figured every man carrying a newspaper was suspect. I manoeuvred myself against a pole so that no one could get at my butt with a stiletto.

By the time we got out at Tsim Sha Tsui Station, I was sweating up a storm. It felt good to shake off the anxiety and breathe in the polluted air when we emerged onto Nathan Road.

As we walked the congested pavement towards the Peninsula Hotel, I admitted to Nick, "Suzie turned up."

"You're kidding me?... You're amazing, mate. So, what happened?"

"We went up to the room and did it like teenagers for two hours."

"I'd never have believed she'd be the type to do that," Nick said, wide-eyed and disbelieving.

"I must admit, it stirred the old worry juices hearing Ian talk about retribution for sleeping with a Triad's girl."

"Why? Wait a minute, is she—?"

"Well, she told me she's sort of imprisoned by someone, so I assumed ... you know, with her being a stunner and all that, it might be someone from the club... someone high up..." I said dully.

"You're thinking she might be the girl of some high-ranking gangster?" he rasped.

"Um, yes, I suppose I am."

"Didn't you think to ask her?"

"Well, I didn't want to spoil the moment... you know...?"

"Axis, your lower head overruling your upper head is very likely to get you... us... into deep trouble."

We entered the Pen lobby.

"No, I don't think so. How would he find out?... Anyhow, we'll be out of here in a couple of days... nothing will come of it... it was just an aberration."

We entered the elevator. The moment after I pushed the button and the doors closed, the elevator gave a cultured sigh and came to rest at our floor.

"I wouldn't think someone like that would take too well to a Gweilo doing the business, if he, per se, was to find out," said Nick, after silently mulling it over for the entire elevator ride.

"Don't be a racist," I snapped jokingly.

"I mean it Axis, the guy Ian told us about was a Gweilo."

Once again, a shiver ran up my spine causing the hairs on the back of my neck to stand at attention.

We both had a little afternoon siesta and woke at 9 P.M. Nick ordered us room service and the customary exceptional service had the food on a table in front of us within twenty minutes. I picked up a French fry and, chewing it, gazed out the window at the Hong Kong skyline. The night was clear and Hong Kong was lit up like a fairyland.

"Mate, I don't feel comfortable about going to the club unarmed. What about you?" I grated.

"I haven't been with Suzie, so I'm not sure I have the same degree of concern as you."

"It's not that, as much as I have this gut feeling… you know what I'm saying? When I get it, I have to listen."

Nick raised a single black eyebrow. "Danger, you sense danger?"

"I feel anxious… so yeah, I, I guess it's probably danger."

"Well, there's not much we can do about it mate, this is not Manila or Sydney, we can't get you a gun… we'll just have to rely on Mark. Do you feel okay about him?"

I thought about it for a second or two then replied truthfully, "I don't know, something feels uncomfortable… can't quite put my finger on it."

"You know I once dropped an expensive gold cufflink from my shirt when I was walking back to my room here at the Peninsula. When I discovered it missing, I rang the reception and ten minutes later a bellhop turned up with it."

"Did he find it?" I asked.

"No, they just replayed the video of me walking up the corridor to my room and saw it drop."

It suddenly dawned on me what he was saying.

"They would have video of Suzie visiting me. Damn right they would, I should have known better!" I cursed.

"That's what I'm saying Axis, when it comes to your lower head taking control, you lose your rationale. I think that's what you're feeling mate… subconsciously you know damn well you've dropped your guard. Someone could be studying that video right now."

"You're right, Nick."

"Was it worth it?"

"She was spectacular!"

"That's not what I asked."

~ ~ ~

A few hours later, we were getting out of a taxi at Temple Street. There seemed to be fewer people around than the night before, perhaps because the weather had taken a turn, and it was drizzling.

When we entered the club, there was a notable difference as well—it was empty. There was not a soul, only a barman and the two goons standing beside the door at the end of the room. This time, they let us pass without question and we approached the red peephole door. Same routine, it opened, but not to whom I expected. It wasn't Suzie; in fact, it wasn't even a female. He led us inside. There were only eight at the table playing cards and no sign of Mark. We sat at the same table as before and ordered the same drinks from the waiter. It was going to be a long night without Suzie to flirt with and no Mark. The atmosphere made me nervous.

"Something's wrong here," I whispered to Nick.

"Yes, it feels claustrophobic."

The waiter returned with the drinks. Nick asked him in Chinese if Mark was expected. When he left, I asked what he'd said.

"He knows nothing."

About an hour later, Nick's phone rang. When he answered, his face turned pale. He hung up quickly and said, "That was Mark; he told me to get out of here right now!"

Nick signalled the waiter and then paid the bill. We got up and calmly made for the door. None of the poker players paid any attention to us at all. We made it all the way through the club and outside onto the street with our hearts in our throats. We had no idea what we were afraid of, but Nick still had on his frantic face as we gazed through the drizzle up the dark street. We knew that any chance of getting a cab was at least a fifteen-minute walk away. Then, I noticed someone move in the darkness along the street a little. Then, another... I whispered to Nick, "There are guys up ahead hiding, waiting for us."

"What should we do?" he asked nervously.

"We either go back inside or make a run for it," I growled.

"Mark said to get out, so I guess we'd better leg it!"

"Okay, let's run in the opposite direction to them and then cut up to Temple Street."

"Got it," Nick agreed.

"Ready?"

"As ready as I'll ever be."

"Okay, let's go!"

We took off like we were coming out of the blocks for the two hundred meters at the Olympics. As we rounded the corner into Saigon Street, I was in the lead and ran straight into two guys waiting for me in ambush. Both were armed with nunchaku. It was like a Bruce Lee film, with me on the wrong side. I skidded to a halt and shaped up; they were broad but shorter. Nick stopped beside me and copied my pose. There were footsteps from behind. I spotted three rubbish bins and quickly grabbed two lids, handing one to Nick.

"Use it as a shield," I croaked.

I charged one of them and felt the blows of the nunchaku on the metal dustbin lid. I gripped the handle and pushed towards him with all my might to drive him into the wall. I could see his legs below my shield, so I kicked at his shins. That stopped him from striking with the nunchaku and gave me a chance to whack him with the lid. I hit him right on the chin, and it cut his face open. I followed it with a flurry of punches, and he went down. The battle behind me was loud. The guy had bashed Nick's shield so hard it had forced him to his knees. Three more ninjas in black hoodies arrived. I saw a chrome glint in the light of a nearby street lamp—it was off a meat cleaver. I launched my shield at the guy attacking Nick and hit him on the back of the head. It split him open big time, and blood sprayed on my face. It gave Nick the chance to get to his feet; he was shaky. We were surrounded, outnumbered—it didn't look good. They closed on us. Then, out of nowhere, a flash of white, and our assailants began going down one at a time. It was the White Snake. He was on his own and making minced-meat of them. Talk about Bruce Lee; White Snake was something to behold. He was carving them up big time. The guy with the meat cleaver went for him, and Mark kicked it out of his hand and then pulverised his face with a barrage of deadly kicks. The guy hit the deck like a sack of potatoes and lay motionless in a puddle of blood. I was enjoying the spectacle when suddenly the lights went out.

~ ~ ~

When I opened my eyes, I had no idea where I was except being flat on my back looking up at a ceiling light. I sat bolt upright, and it hurt so much I fell back down.

"He's awake," I heard, but didn't recognise the voice.

"Where am I?" I growled, and that hurt as well.

A face I didn't know came into view—a western face—a woman.

"Who are you?" I mumbled.

"I'm Kerry, you're in my apartment."

The accent registered. "You're an Aussie."

"Yes, so are you."

I looked at my body. My shirt was off, and my ribs were bandaged—I was in my underpants. I felt cold.

"Brrr, it's cold."

Kerry covered me with a blanket.

"Sorry, love, but I only just finished bandaging you up when you came around. You took one hell of a beating."

"Is Nick—?"

"Yes, your friend is in the other room. He's in better shape than you, but he's got some bruises and a split eyebrow. He's resting."

"And Mark?"

"Mark!" she called out.

Next, Mark was looking down at me with a cheeky smile.

"You fought well, my friend. I could get you a gig as a stunty," he mumbled, with a chuckle.

"No thanks, I couldn't afford the insurance," I struggled to say. "Anything broken?"

"No, your ribs are just bruised," Mark said. "One of them put the boot in big time while you were on the ground after that bastard king-hit you."

I felt my left ear. It was ringing and hurt like hell.

"Yep, that's where he hit you. Mind you, he blindsided you—you never saw it coming. Kerry stitched your ear up, so it'll be fine, just a war wound," he said.

"Bloody hell, you did a job on them," I rasped.

"I'm only sorry I didn't get there earlier."

"Who the hell were they?"

"I was just telling Nick in there, they were 14K. We got word there was going to be an attack. You guys just happened to walk out of the club smack-bang into it. But listen, a few bumps and bruises, but now the Dragon Head owes you one."

"Yeah, why's that?"

"He was playing poker. He came to meet you and was definitely the target of the 14K attack. You guys stopped the attack, so yeah, he owes you big time."

Seemed we had broken through and made contact. Not exactly how we would have preferred it but nevertheless we'd succeeded, and the way it happened probably put us in even better stead.

"Where am I?"

"This is my friend Kerry's apartment in Mong Kok, not far from the Four Fingers. Lucky she was home and could tend to your wounds, she's a nurse."

"At least she knew what she was doing," I said with a sigh.

"Yeah, she treats animals every day with wounds like yours," he grinned.

"Animals?"

"Yeah, she's a veterinary nurse."

"What!" I complained loudly... and it hurt like hell.

CHAPTER FOURTEEN

I N THE MORNING, a car took us to the Peninsula. We entered our room like the walking dead. Nick ordered coffees from room service and we sat down to chat with Mark.

"Just exactly who is to blame for the attack, Mark," Nick growled.

It wasn't often Nick showed his anger, but in this case, he was seriously agitated.

"It is difficult because the 14K have no Dragon Head. You should have heard of them, Axis, they're very active in Sydney."

"I'm only just learning about this Triad stuff in Sydney, Mark," I grunted, still aching.

"The most likely suspect is Won Kuok-Lim or as he is better known, Broken Teeth-Lim. In 1999, he declared himself Dragon Head of the 14K, but it's rumoured someone within the 14K grassed on him to the cops because factions didn't want a Dragon Head. He was released from prison in 2014 after serving fifteen years for murder and has been making moves to re-take the film industry since. I reckon, he's solely responsible for the increased attacks on Sun Yee On, like last night."

"Does he have the support of the 14K?" Nick asked.

"We think some, but you must understand, the 14K are the enemy of Sun Yee On, and they are extremely violent. It is difficult to find out much about them. But it is speculated that Broken Teeth was behind the assassination of Lee Tai Lung, Dragon Head of Sun

Yee On, outside the Kowloon Shangri La in 2004. That's really all I can say, fellas. I have to go now. You will be contacted."

"Thanks for everything, Mark," I said, taking his hand.

Nick walked him to the door. When he came back, he said, "That was pretty surreal last night, I still don't know what happened. Last thing I remember is you using a rubbish bin lid to crunch a guy belting me with nun-chucks...next minute I woke up this morning with Kerry trying to feed me orange juice through a straw."

"We were lucky to get out of there alive, mate. If it hadn't been for Mark, we would have been minced meat."

"I don't know about you but I feel like minced meat," he said, feeling his cut and swollen eyebrow.

"Those stitches look okay, not a bad job for a veterinary nurse."

The look on his face was priceless.

"A what?" he demanded.

"She treats animals, mate, not much difference I suppose...look, she stitched my ear up...did an okay job, didn't she?"

Nick took a look. "Yes, I suppose she did."

~ ~ ~

We rested all day, and by nightfall, after a bottle of JD to reduce the pain, we were both feeling a lot better. Nick had spoken to Ty and told him what had happened, he repeated his warning to leave the 14K alone and to focus on Sun Yee On. When Nick questioned his reasoning, he simply said 14K have a strong presence in Sydney and Manila, and it wouldn't be worth making enemies of them. Nick suggested the beating we took meant we were never going to be friends. Ty reckoned we might have got off lightly.

Just after 8 P.M., we got a call from the front desk to say there were three gentlemen to see us. Feeling nervous as to whom it might be, Nick asked for one of them to be put on the phone. He spoke to him in Cantonese then hung up.

"I told them to come up," he said, "they're friends of White Snake."

"Quick, ring Mark and ask if this is normal," I said hurriedly.

Nick dialled Mark. "Message bank, what do you want to do?"

"You show them in," I said, jumping up and slipping behind the door.

There was a knock. I winked at Nick, he opened the door and showed them in. I let them pass then stuck my finger in the middle of the last guy's back and ordered, "Hold it right there … hands up."

He froze and slowly raised his hands. The other two stopped, went to turn and face me.

"Keep looking straight ahead!" I growled. "Nick, frisk them."

Nick patted them down one at a time.

"They're clean," Nick said sternly.

"Okay, you can lower your hands, the three of you sit down," I demanded, keeping my hand in my pocket pretending that I had a gun. "You." I picked the more regal-looking of the three. "Who are you and what do you want?"

"My name is Lee Kok Lung, Mr Stone," he said calmly and soft-spoken. "I am Dragon Head of Sun Yee On. This is Red Pole, Fatty Tung and with his hands half-raised in submission, White Paper Fan, Soy Ling Chu. We are here because White Snake informed us you wanted to meet to discuss the debts of Sun Ty."

Nick spoke up diplomatically, "I am Nick Vargas."

"I know of you, Mr Vargas …" he said, and then carried on in Cantonese.

"I think it would be best to speak English for Mr Stone's benefit," Nick said diplomatically.

The threat had passed, so I gestured for us all to take a seat.

"You can lower your hands," I growled.

"Your finger is not like a .38 Mr Stone," Soy said with an icy smirk.

"Last night I wished it was a .38, it would have saved us from a beating."

I didn't recognise any of them from the poker table last night. Lee was around forty-five I guessed, with thick black hair peppered with grey, and an air of obvious authority. His eyes were deep-set, and black, his lips were thin, set in a straight line. Soy and Tung, on the other hand, were a bit younger and less well-groomed. Tung was tubby with a moon face, while Soy was skinny and rat-faced.

"We are very grateful for your brave stand last night, Mr Stone and Mr Vargas," Fatty said, with a strong accent.

This guy had a distrustful glint in his eye that I didn't take to at all.

"And we are thankful for the courage of White Snake," Nick countered.

"He has been a valued servant to us for many years," Lee admitted.

"Let's cut to the chase, Mr Lee," I said challengingly.

Soy answered on his behalf. "Mr Lee is prepared to waive the debt for a half governing share in the Golden Dragon restaurant. Ty Sun would still head-up the company, but without the deciding vote. In addition, Ty will work with a manager appointed by Sun Yee On."

I looked at Nick and he raised his eyebrows. I nodded for him to continue.

"What happens if Ty Sun and his family reject the offer?" Nick asked.

"Then he must pay up," Soy snapped.

"And how much is that, Mr Soy?"

"Two million in gambling debts and of course repayment for the money stolen in 1947—"

Nick cut him off. "Mr Sun can attest for the gambling debt but there is no record of any debt from 1947. I'm afraid it dwells only in the world of myth."

"All legend has a base in fact, Mr Vargas, so if Mr Sun would like to settle the debts, we will establish in the total, an estimated figure for the 1947 debt."

"And if he doesn't agree to any of these terms, Mr Lee?" I questioned, eyeballing him.

"Then things could become very unpleasant for Mr Sun and his family," Soy answered.

"My question wasn't directed at you, Soy," I said, keeping my eyes locked on Lee.

"He speaks for me, Mr Stone," Lee said with an expressionless tone.

"This isn't really a business discussion, it's extortion," I growled, staring Soy down.

"Call it what you like, Stone: it is how we do business," Fatty Tung snarled at me.

There was a pause for the smouldering tempers to chill.

"What are your plans in Sydney?" I asked calmly.

"The 14K have infiltrated the film industry and drug trafficking there — they have forged an alliance with 5T, a Vietnamese organisation — together they plan to take over the Chinese gambling business controlled by Sun Yee On. We will stop them by whatever means necessary," Soy said zealously.

"What has owning a restaurant got to do with that?" I growled back at him.

"Together with Fortune Garden, the Golden Dragon will add to our influence within the Chinese business community," Lee suggested diplomatically.

"We will need to discuss your proposition with Ty," Nick said.

"It would be best to meet on my junk, 'Tai Lung' at Aberdeen at 7 P.M., for dinner and hopefully … a resolution," Lee said, rising ready to leave.

"I don't like boats," I complained.

"The Tai Lung is moored, Mr Stone, it won't be going anywhere."

We shook hands with each of them and they left. I poured a couple of drinks then Nick and I sat down to discuss the deal.

"I got serious bad vibes from Soy Ling, I don't trust him. What's a bloody White Paper Fan anyway?" I admitted.

"I think he's an administrator, like an accountant, and Fatty Tung is a Red Pole, an enforcer," Nick explained.

"Ah, so Fatty is the muscle and Soy the brains?"

"I guess you could say that."

"How do you think Ty will take the offer," I asked.

"By the sound of it, they're not giving him much choice, but he'd sooner lose control of the company than lose face or his life."

"I think you better phone him, he might need some time to mull it over," I suggested.

Nick drew his smartphone and dialled. Just then the house phone rang. I answered — it was Suzie — she was in the lobby.

I left Nick on the phone to Ty, and went down to meet her.

~ ~ ~

I found her sitting alone at a table. "Hey Suzie," I said, taking a chair opposite her. She peeled off her sunglasses and looked at me with a horrified stare.

"What happened to your face, Axis?"

"I was on the wrong side of a fight last night. That reminds me, why weren't you at the club?"

She looked incredibly attractive, dressed in a just-above-the-knee navy blue skirt and a brown jacket over a beige blouse. Her legs were bare and inviting. She crossed them when she noticed me staring.

"I was told not to come to work last night because there would be trouble," she said flatly.

"Yeah, well, the trouble found me. Who told you that?"

She looked down, embarrassed, "My boyfriend...he arranged the attack, I'm sure...I heard him talking on the phone. It was staged to frighten both of you."

"Staged? What! Who is this guy? You've got to tell me, babe."

"His name is Soy Ling Chu," she said disconsolately.

"Soy! The White Paper Fan!"

"You know him?" she said, surprised.

"He just left us no more than twenty minutes ago. You're lucky he didn't see you!"

She bit her bottom lip and looked around anxiously.

"Axis, I came here to warn you not to go to the meeting on the junk. If things don't go their way, they will kill you. I overheard Soy telling Fatty Tung."

"I don't believe this. Where? How?" I questioned.

"I was in the car this morning when he was talking to Fatty."

As she grew more upset, her English began to falter. She stood up, looking extremely nervous.

"I must leave. If Soy find me gone, he beat me."

"You risked your life to warn me? Thank you." I stood and kissed her gently on the lips, then wiped away a tear trickling down her pale cheek.

"Please be safe, Axis. I want see you again," she said softly.

~ ~ ~

He was reading the newspaper when I stormed into the room.

"It was a set-up!" I snarled.

He put down the paper. "Sit down. What do you mean?"

"That was Suzie. You won't believe this, her boyfriend is Soy, the White Paper Fan... he warned her yesterday not to go to work at the Four Fingers because there would be trouble. She said it was staged to frighten us."

"What?" Nick bleated. "You've got to be kidding."

"Yes, but what's more, she overheard Soy telling Fatty Tung in the car this morning that if things go wrong on the Junk tonight, they're going to kill us."

"Holy hell!" Nick bellowed. "That also means Mark's in on it with them and can't be trusted."

"What did Ty say?"

"He needs time to think it over, like you thought — his first reaction was no. He'll call back later with a decision. Now, I see the value of your liaison with Suzie. I'm sorry to have doubted you."

"I don't think we've got much choice with this, mate... we're going to need the cops."

CHAPTER FIFTEEN

I RANG THE OCTB at the Hong Kong police and asked for my contact: Detective Inspector Shun Zhong. It took a couple of minutes, but eventually, I was transferred to his cell phone. When he answered, I told him who I was and that DI Malone had given me his name. I explained what had happened the previous night, outlined the meeting we'd just had, and expressed our fear for our safety after what Suzie had told me. He told us to stay put; he was only half an hour away.

I answered the door to DI Zhong. He didn't resemble a cop, nothing like what I'd anticipated. Dressed in smart casual attire, he looked a lot like a younger version of Chow Yun-fat of "Crouching Tiger Hidden Dragon" fame. I introduced myself and then took him over to meet Nick. We sat down to talk.

"Can I get you anything?" I asked.

"No, I'm fine, thank you."

His English was excellent, and given his early forties age, it was easy to tell he'd been through some tough battles... Scars dissected both eyebrows, and there was a coldness about him that only comes from having seen and done terrible things.

"Can you tell us anything about these guys, Lee Kok Lung, Fatty Tung, and Soy Ling Chu?" Nick asked.

"They are the big Triad — Lee Kok Lung is Dragon Head of Sun Yee On. He is the eldest son of Lee Tai Lung who, as Dragon Head, was assassinated in 2004. Lee Kok took power as Dragon Head in

2006 after he graduated from a Sydney university. His younger brother, Lee Kit Wo, believed to be currently studying in Sydney, is ten years younger. As for Fatty Tung, he has a record as long as your arm, as does his sidekick, Soy Ling Chu. I've personally been trying to bring those two down for the last ten years."

"Could the younger brother be Dragon Head of the Sydney chapter of Sun Yee On?" I questioned.

"Could be, but we don't have much intelligence on that chapter, as you would understand."

"I ask because if things go wrong here, there will be reprisals in Sydney, and we don't want to put the Sun family in any more danger," I explained.

"The family should be put under protection until this is over," he said unyieldingly.

"You're right, Shun. Is that what I should call you?" I asked.

"No, call me Zhong."

"What's your view of this meeting scheduled tonight?" Nick queried.

"You can trust the warning Suzie gave you because she is the girlfriend of Soy. Though we must ask why she has warned you."

"We had intimate relations," I admitted.

"Okay, that explains it but makes it even more problematic. You are lucky she has taken a liking to you, Axis. She might have saved your life."

"I appreciate that, Zhong," I said, shaking my head at the close call.

"What about Mark, White Snake?" Nick asked.

"He's one of their enforcers. Stay away from him; he plays both sides of the fence for them," he said seriously. "Tonight, you will need to go in armed and with back up. I know the Junk; we've had it under surveillance for some time. I can't go in with you, we can't get a warrant — it would be too dangerous for anyone to accompany you. Irrespective of what Ty Sun decides, you know there will be serious consequences — it's only a matter of whether you want to confront them here or in Sydney."

"Are you suggesting to tell them what they want to hear, then deal with it in Sydney?" I posed.

"Yes. The alternative is to bring it to a head tonight, have a shootout, and still have to deal with it in Sydney."

"With all your experience with the Triads, what would you do in our shoes, Zhong?" Nick asked.

"If it was the 14K, you would have to fight right here and then again in Australia. But being Sun Yee On, I'd agree to their terms, then I'd get to the younger brother and make it clear he'll go down if a threat is made to any member of the Sun family."

"Then what? … Pay the money and give them control of the restaurant?" Nick questioned.

"I think gaining the upper hand is the answer, and you won't be able to do that here, but you could in Sydney. Ty Sun is no fool; he is a very astute businessman. He will know exactly what to do once he has attained the power position in negotiations," Zhong maintained.

"Whoa, that's Chinese logic for you…" I said, struggling to make sense of it.

"Very sensible," said Nick, then added a few paragraphs in Cantonese. By the expression on his face, Zhong was surprised Nick was so fluent. I let them chat while I poured myself a glass of bourbon.

"Axis," Nick called out, "I'm going to phone Ty now to get his decision. I'll then explain the plan Zhong has outlined. Okay by you?"

I sauntered back over to them, sat down, took a sip of my drink, and then acknowledged, "Yep, that's the right move."

Nick dialled Ty and spoke in Cantonese. After a few minutes, he handed the phone to Zhong, who continued the conversation for another few minutes.

"Zhong is explaining the idea in more detail," Nick told me.

"What's his decision?"

"Ironically, he'd drawn the same conclusion," Nick said. "There's nothing to gain here except accepting the deal. The rest needs to be fought out in Sydney."

"I'd better give Malone a call and put a heavy watch on Jazz and Ty."

"Good thinking," Nick agreed.

While Zhong was still talking to Ty, I phoned Rick and filled him in. He reminded me I'd not sent him the incriminating photo of Grant Lee and Chiang. I apologized and promised to get it to him upon my return. I asked if he could do me one last favour … check police records and find out if Grant Lee is his full name. He agreed, stating it wouldn't take him long and that he would text me the result. In closing, he asked me to bring back a present from Hong Kong and to watch my back. I hung up at the same time Zhong did.

"I've arranged with Sydney Homicide for surveillance of Ty Sun and his daughter, Jazz," I announced.

"Good, that's one part of the puzzle solved," Nick said.

"How was your discussion with Ty?" I asked Zhong.

"He's fine; he agreed totally with the MO. He knows more than I expected about the ways of Sun Yee On, and he agrees he'd rather have them as an enemy than the 14K, but at the same time he knows having either of them as enemies is not a desirable outcome," Zhong explained.

"Well, unfortunately, you make your bed and you have to lie in it?" I said philosophically.

"Very good, Axis. With Confucian quotes like that, we'll make an Asian out of you yet," Zhong joked.

"Don't worry, from the last case he had in Manila, he's practically an honorary Filipino!" Nick wisecracked.

"If we live through tonight, I'll expect the same from here," I added.

Zhong reached inside his coat and produced a holstered .38 and handed it to me.

"Here, you'll be needing this. It's unregistered, not police issue — I didn't give it to you, but I want it back, preferably unfired. Nick, are you okay with being unarmed?"

"You bet. Happy to leave that to Axis," Nick replied.

I saw Zhong out. We had an MO; now all we needed to do was pull it off without stopping a bullet.

A few minutes later, my phone sounded an incoming text.

"From Rick," I said. "I'd asked him for Grant Lee's full name on police records. It's Lee Kit Wo. Isn't that the name of the younger brother to Lee Kok Lung?"

"Sure is."

"Now we can safely say the Dragon Head of the Sydney chapter of Sun Yee On is Grant Lee, a detective in the vice squad."

"It's a definite advantage knowing Grant Lee is the Dragon Head's brother, and you're doing the right thing by keeping that a secret here," Nick said.

"That's exactly what I'm telling Rick," I said, typing my reply to his text.

~ ~ ~

The early afternoon had me needing rest and repair for the big event coming later. Nick bailed out to trawl the malls for a present for Kitty, so I kicked back to watch ESPN. It struck me: if it all goes tits-up tonight and Zhong and his men have to make a stand, Soy will know it was Suzie who blew the whistle on him. Going on what she'd said about him, it would be like signing her death warrant. With no means of contacting her, I racked my brain on how to save her. Then I noticed Zhong's calling card on the coffee table. I immediately dialled his cellphone and laid the problem on him. He said there was nothing we could do for her... we just had to hope nothing goes wrong and then no-one would be hurt. I knew he was right; I guess I'd panicked.

~ ~ ~

At first glance, Aberdeen gave me the impression it was like the 21st Century meets the 19th Century, with thirty-story skyscrapers hugging the foreshore, looking down at a view of stacks and stacks of Junks anchored in the bay. I could see why they were called Junks: most of them were like something someone had thrown out. As soon as I stepped out of the taxi at the wharf, the stench hit me — whoa, was it ripe! It seemed more than Junks had been dumped in the water. A faint lapping sound got louder as we walked along the wharf towards what we figured to be the Tai Lung, moored at the end.

"I'm still not thrilled about going on that bloody thing," I grumbled to Nick.

"You won't get seasick; it's moored... unless of course a massive storm hits," he looked up, "and that's unlikely, it's not the rainy season."

"Thanks mate, that makes me feel so much better," I said facetiously.

"Someday Soon" played two bars then stopped. It was the pre-agreed signal from Zhong, that he and his men were in position for us to board the Tai Lung.

As foul as the air was, the harbour was lit up like a fairyland. But I wasn't in the mood for taking in the view; tonight was about self-preservation.

A huge six-story barge painted in rich colours and decorated all over with lights was floating out in the middle of the bay, with a big green neon sign saying Jumbo on its upper deck.

"What's Jumbo floating out there?" I asked Nick.

"It's a famous floating restaurant. You catch that water ferry over there out to it. When you order seafood on board, you select what you want from a huge variety of live fish, lobsters, crabs, and abalone in on-board tanks."

"Wait," I stopped him, and held up my phone to pose for a selfie with the Jumbo in the background. "One more." I positioned the Tai Lung behind us. "Cool, I hope we get to look back on them in years to come."

"So do I," Nick agreed.

I'm sure we both had knots in our guts. It's not easy to walk into a set-up knowing you might not walk out of it.

We were close to the Junk. I looked down at a smaller boat moored at the side of the wharf and caught sight of Zhong on it — that was a relief. I pouted my lips Filipino style to Nick in the direction of Zhong, and he seemed equally encouraged.

The rotund form of Fatty Tung appeared on the deck of the Tai Lung and waved us aboard. We followed him down a companionway into the main cabin where we found Lee and Soy seated at a round table, similar to the poker table at the Four Fingers. As a matter of fact, the interior of the Junk was decked out as lavishly as the gaming room at the Four Fingers, and surprisingly spacious. Lee rose to his feet but not Soy.

"Gentlemen, good to see you, please be seated at my table," he said happily, as he filled a small cup in front of each of us with tea from a pot. I took a sip, it was Jasmine.

"Tasty," I said, eyeballing Soy who was busy avoiding eye contact. I watched Fatty sit and felt comfortable that only the five of us were present.

CHAPTER SIXTEEN

❝YOU HAVE A nice Junk, Mr Lee. How old is she?" Nick asked.

"She belonged to my father and carries his name," he replied calmly. "He built her in 1950."

"How long were you in Sydney?" I asked.

For a split second, I had the rare experience of looking into a man's eyes and seeing a true reflection of his thoughts. The ice-cold ferocity of his hate hit me almost physically; then, in the next instant, it vanished, and his eyes returned to normal—just like the eyes of a feral animal.

"I compliment you on doing your homework, Mr Stone. I completed a four-year degree in business strategy at the University of New South Wales," he said.

"Almost an Aussie then, are we?" I added sarcastically.

"I like to think so. I have many friends in Sydney."

"And a brother, of course—" I probed a little deeper.

Soy cut me off rudely. "Let's get on with the business at hand."

There was a pause while I drilled Lee with a cold, hard stare, just to let him know I was annoyed by Soy's indignant interruption.

"You'll have to pardon Soy, Mr Stone. He has another appointment soon in Mong Kok."

Nick coughed to get attention and spoke up to cool things down. "I have spoken with Ty Sun, and he has authorised me to accept your terms of offer."

"Not good enough, Mr Vargas," Soy snapped.

"Isn't that what we agreed?" Nick responded indignantly.

"I think Soy is saying we don't trust you. Nothing personal," Fatty Tung growled testily with a wry smile. "But we need to hear it from the horse's mouth."

I could tell by his expression that Nick was offended. He moved sharply to reach into his jacket for his cellphone. Fatty and Soy flinched, thinking he was pulling a gun. I noticed by their hand movements that they were both armed. They relaxed when Nick showed them his phone.

"You can see by the ID that I'm dialling Ty Sun," he said, displaying the phone and then putting it up to his ear. "Hello, Ty. It's Nick—" He switched the phone to speaker mode and continued speaking in Cantonese. After a few sentences, he handed the phone over to Lee, who continued the conversation in Cantonese. All the while, I was eyeballing Soy; he made my skin crawl.

Lee finished the call and handed Nick back his phone. They spoke in Cantonese, then eventually reverted to English.

"I am satisfied with the arrangements," Lee confirmed to me.

"Too easy," I said and stood up from the table.

"Sit down, Mr Stone," Soy growled. "We haven't finished yet."

I glared back, irritated by his surly attitude.

"What's your problem, Soy? You're acting like you missed out on getting an after-dinner mint?" I retorted.

He stood slowly and confronted me. "I don't like you, Stone."

"Well, you know what? I don't like you more. Now, are we done here or what?" I glared past Soy at Lee.

Soy and I had squared off like a pair of prizefighters at a weigh-in press conference.

"You're just a waste of space," I challenged.

He shook his head contemptuously.

Nick rushed to the rescue. "Is there something more you wish to discuss, Mr Lee?" he asked in a mild tone.

"I don't think so, Mr Vargas," Lee said easily. "I think you should leave now," he announced before I had a chance to open my mouth.

Soy sank back into his seat, and a hoarse whisper in Chinese escaped him. It had a frightening undercurrent of tension hovering around the breaking point; I guessed he was sore.

I waited a couple of beats for added impact, staring down Soy. Then, when Nick shook hands with Lee and Fatty, I followed suit but bypassed Soy, out of distaste.

"We won't be staying for dinner, then? Thanks for the tea," I said cynically.

I let Nick lead the way out.

We got up onto the deck, and Nick climbed onto the wharf. Then I heard my name shouted out loud and urgently. "Stone, look out!"

I looked up sharply to see Zhong. He was standing at the edge of the wharf with his arms extended, a pistol gripped in both hands and aimed at me. Bang! He fired, and I heard a loud thump hit the deck behind me. I swivelled around sharply to see Soy on the deck with a bullet hole in his chest, taking his last gasp of air while blood frothed from his snarling mouth. Next to his hand on the floorboards lay the .38 he was about to shoot me with when Zhong spotted him. A thunderous roar, like a charging rhino, preceded Fatty emerging onto the deck with a gun in hand and a face as red as a beetroot.

I whipped out my .38 and shoved it in his face. "Forget it, Fatso!" I ordered, and he dropped the gun like it was a hot potato. Cops appeared from everywhere. Three of them leapt onto the Junk; two tackled Fatty, and the other cuffed his hands behind his back.

I climbed onto the wharf and immediately shook Zhong's hand. "Thank you, my friend. I guess I owe you a drink."

"The pleasure was all mine, Axis. Any excuse to take out that bastard."

"I won't be needing this anymore. Thanks," I said, handing over the gun he'd given me.

"What are you going to do about Lee? He's still on board," Nick asked Zhong.

"He knows we can't touch him without a search warrant. He'll just sit tight making calls to arrange bail for Fatty."

"You can't charge Fatty?" Nick asked.

"No. With what? Carrying an illegal firearm? He'd get off that in a flash. No, the only time we ever win is when we catch one of them in the act of committing a serious crime. With your help tonight, we at least managed to eliminate one of them. Can I give you a lift back to the Pen?" Zhong asked casually.

"Yeah, appreciate that, mate," I said.

"What, don't you want to have dinner on the Jumbo?" Nick asked with a smug look on his face.

"You'll not get me on another boat, mate," I jeered. "Every time I go near one of those bloody things, I nearly get killed."

Nick laughed as we followed Zhong to his unmarked police car.

~ ~ ~

We bid goodbye to Zhong inside the car out front of the Pen.

"I'll need a statement from both of you. Can you draft it tonight and email me?" Zhong asked.

"No worries, mate, cheers," I said, shaking his hand.

"We'll probably fly out to Sydney tomorrow morning, so until next time," Nick said, reaching over from the back seat to take Zhong's hand.

"You've got my contact details, so keep me updated on how you get on," Zhong said.

We got out and went into the hotel.

I flopped into a chair in the room.

"Well," I said with a sigh, "we live to fight another day."

Nick sat opposite with his head in his hands. "I'm going to have to start getting paid for these gigs."

"Surely you don't need the money?"

"I'll need a lot more to pay my insurance if this keeps up," he chuckled.

"Maybe we should be partners... Stone and Vargas — a private detective agency... sounds pretty cool."

"I think I might make old bones if I don't take you up on that offer, mate," Nick said with a facetious chuckle.

The house phone rang, and Nick was closest, so he answered it.

"Hello, oh, hi, yes, one moment." He covered the receiver with his hand and whispered, "It's Suzie."

I nodded to take it, and he handed me the phone.

"Hi, yes, I'm all right, but not Soy. He tried to shoot me and got himself killed." The phone fell silent while she processed the news. I glanced at Nick.

He whispered, "She'll need to get out of town. Tell her we'll arrange for her to stay at my house in Manila. There's a Cathay flight to Manila tomorrow morning at nine and one to Sydney at the same time."

He was right... it was the safest course of action. No doubt Fatty would come after her once he got out of clink. I told her, and she was relieved. "I'll get you an air ticket, don't worry. Do you want to stay here tonight?" I asked. She couldn't, too much to take care of — it was going to be a drastic life change for her. I wasn't really up for her tonight anyway, aching all over.

"What's her full name?" Nick asked.

"What's your full name, babe... for the ticket? Suzie Wong, I should have seen that one coming," I joked. "Okay, so, meet me in the Peninsula lobby at 7 A.M. Yes, then we can go to the airport together. Okay? Don't be late. Bye." I hung up, not really convinced she was safe.

Nick looked up from studying his iPhone. "I've booked CX901 to Manila for Suzie Wong, and we're booked on CX139."

"Good, what's our ETA?" I asked.

"Um, 8 P.M. subject to winds, of course."

"Thanks for helping out with her, Nick," I said graciously.

"Hey, what are friends for? If it hadn't been for her, we could have been killed tonight. I'll just put it on the bill."

Chuckling at his gag, I struggled up and staggered over to the bar to make myself a drink.

"I'll just text driver Dom to pick her up at the airport... whatever you're having, I'll take one as well."

That was a turn up; Nick rarely indulged. I poured two neat two-finger bourbons and added a few cubes.

"I feel like I've been through the mincer," I said, carrying the drinks back, walking like an octogenarian. "You better give Kitty a call and tell her you're okay."

"Good thinking, I'll do that. Why don't you ring Jazz to let her know we survived," he said, taking a glass from me.

"I'll do that right after I guzzle this lovely drink. Cheers to cheating death yet again, Mr Vargas." I toasted.

We clinked glasses.

"Ahh, the best pain relief I know," I said, satisfied.

I couldn't sleep, even after half a dozen JD's, I was just too worried about Suzie. Around 2 A.M., I dropped a sleeping pill; the next minute, I felt someone shaking my shoulder, and I sat up in bed with a jolt. It was Nick, and it was 6 A.M. time to rise.

Glaring at my reflection in the mirror while trying to shave, I found it difficult to raise my left arm due to the bruised ribs. As for my face, the black and blue bruising had come out — along with the torn and stitched-up left ear, it made me look like I'd just been a round in the ring with Tim Tszyu.

Nick's the perfect bloke to travel with; he's so together and neat, it stinks. While I was in the bathroom going through my morning ablutions, he'd ordered breakfast and fixed the bill, so all I had to do was pack my port, and I was ready to rock. We threw down a croissant and a cup of coffee and then headed down to the lobby.

~ ~ ~

There wasn't much activity there at 7 A.M., just a couple of those types you always see in hotels wearing a headband and lycra, off for a jog in the pollution... and then a few like us with bags under their eyes and at their feet, checking out.

Nick went out to the forecourt to supervise the loading of the limo while I sat in a lobby chair, on the lookout for Suzie.

Every now and then, I checked the clock on the wall behind reception. It was now 7:15, and I was beginning to worry. When it got to 7:25, I sighted Nick making his way toward me, and I figured he wasn't going to be able to hold the limo much longer.

"We've got to go, Axis," Nick said sorrowfully.

"I hear you." Feeling glum, I picked myself up, grabbed my port, and walked slowly toward the main doors where the limo waited on the other side.

CHAPTER SEVENTEEN

I**'D JUST REACHED** the big double glass front doors of the Peninsula when I heard a small voice at the back of me call my name. I turned so sharply it hurt. It was Suzie, struggling with two big bags, hustling her way from the eastern entrance. I thanked heaven, even though I'm agnostic.

Nick was relieved to see us make our way to the Roller. It was another sultry day — misty rain, and not even rainy season — I was glad to be leaving, even though I never really got a taste of this fantastic city. We climbed into the Roller.

"Nick, you know Suzie," I said.

"Hi Nick, Axis told me 'bout you," she said, coyly. "I remember you from Four Fingers."

"I only told her the good stuff, Nick," I said with a chuckle.

"So, we go Manila?" she asked, dropping her prepositions.

"Um, no, you're going to Manila," I said with a frown.

She looked down like she was about to cry.

"But I don't know anyone and have no money to find a—"

Nick chimed in, "It's okay, Suzie. We owe you plenty for saving our lives... you're most welcome to stay at my house for as long as you like. My driver Dom will collect you from the airport."

"Where you go, Axis?" she asked with a single tear traversing her pale cheek.

"Sydney... we have business to do there," I told her.

"Axis lives there, Suzie, but I live in Manila. I will be in Australia for a couple of months, then back to Manila," Nick explained carefully.

She understood, but still had those sad, lost puppy dog eyes. So, Nick expanded on what he had been saying in Cantonese, and that seemed to brighten her up.

It was a sombre trip to the airport, the weather outside the limo was gloomy, the feeling inside the limo just as gloomy. I looked down at Suzie's red shoes — they reminded me of Dorothy in the Wizard of Oz. I looked out of the window and saw her reflection — her ruby red lips, her black shoulder-length hair with a kick of natural curl that gave it life and lift.

"Next time you come to Hong Kong, Axis, make it spring, it's lovely then," Nick said. "We can play golf... I've got an actor friend with a helicopter, we could have had some fun dropping in on some of the islands to play."

"Hitting the islands would be fun, but the golf with all things maritime... is a no-no for Axis Stone, I'm afraid. Last time I played golf, it was at Bonnie Doon in Sydney. I played so lousy I threw my clubs into a lake and walked off the course... I've not played since. I'm left-handed and play right-handed... get that."

"Pros say that's the best combination, it means your strongest arm pulls through the shot," he explained, imitating the motion with his hands.

"That'd be fine if I could hit the ball in the right direction... I'd need a GPS in the bloody thing to find it. That last game? I think by the fourth hole, I'd lost six balls."

It was an even more depressing scene at the airport. It felt like I'd known Suzie for ages. I hate goodbyes, and this was an Academy Award-winning performance... she clung to me sobbing like a child. I promised to call her regularly and that I would come and see her soon. By the time we boarded our flight, I was emotionally exhausted.

~ ~ ~

I slept like a baby most of the way to Sydney and missed out on indulging in the wonderful Cathay Pacific first-class treatment, though the stewardess gently covered me in a blanket once I'd curled up in the big comfy seat to sleep. I did, however, get to treat myself to a perfect Harvey Wallbanger and a plate of scrumptious hors-d'oeuvres before we touched down in good ol' Sydney town.

~ ~ ~

There was no reason for Nick to stay in Sydney, so he decided to catch a domestic flight to Brisbane.

"You going to be able to handle this without your trusty sidekick?" he questioned with a snigger.

"Yes, Tonto, I can deal with it."

We hugged as good mates do, and as I watched him head for the domestic terminal bus, I bellowed after him, "Hi-Yo, Silver!"

That turned a lot of heads, and a young boy about eight years old cruised over to me, put his hands on his hips, and complained pugnaciously, "Hey, you're not the Lone Ranger! Anyhow, it's 'Hi-ho, Silver, Away!' not 'Hi-yo, Silver!'... and where's your mask?"

"Go check your Wikipedia, son," I said, pulling a COVID mask from my pocket and waving it under his nose. "Here's my mask, couldn't wear it through customs, they'd have thought I was a terrorist," I said, doing my best Lone Ranger impression.

He went running back to his mother, screaming, "Terrorist! Mum, that man over there is a terrorist!"

Fearing I might get arrested, I quickly hopped in a cab for the city. I'm convinced there's a definite disconnect between me and kids.

~ ~ ~

It felt good to be back in my flat. I immediately went to my secret whippy and retrieved Rosy's iPod. I flopped onto the lounge to work out how to get the photo of Grant Lee and Chiang off the device, so

I could send it to Rick. I gave up and decided I'd better ask someone tech-savvy like Jazz. I was just about to phone her when the intercom buzzed. I answered — it was Jazz — I buzzed her up. I put the iPod back and quickly tidied up the flat. My ribs killed me with every bend; I needed a few painkillers.

A knock at the door sent me to open it. I flung it open ready to give her a big hug and copped a punch in the face. The force reeled me backwards, and I hit the floor, banging my head so hard it very nearly knocked me out. Blinking my eyes, trying to stay conscious, I peered up through the flying stars at two burly guys standing over me, their faces distorted by stockings covering their heads. They looked surreal, but the reality was that one of them had a gun pointed at my face, with the other one brandishing a baseball bat.

The guy with the gun ordered, "Get up."

I wasn't about to argue and struggled to my feet, holding my throbbing jaw. Another guy pushed Jazz ahead of him through the door. The three of them were Chinese. I'm sure one of them was the big guy that whacked me in the office a week ago.

The guy holding Jazz savagely pushed her onto the lounge, then barked at her in Cantonese, I guess to stay put, while he viciously gagged her. Her face looked pale, panicked, her normally neat and tidy appearance all roughed up. But to her credit, she wasn't whimpering. To the contrary, she had a look in her eye that given half the chance, she'd rip her attacker's head off. We exchanged a glance, and her eyes softened for me.

Whack! A pistol smacked me in the temple and sent my head reeling.

"Where is the photo?" The guy who'd whacked me demanded through clenched teeth with a heavily accented voice.

"What photo!" I snapped back at him, as a tepid rivulet of blood trickled down my cheek from a cut in my head.

"Okay, have it your way, Gweilo! Hold her!" he aggressively ordered, and the two guys grabbed Jazz by the arms.

He commanded angrily, "Lift her!"

They rough-handled her to her feet. She struggled against their grip, but there was no point; they were too strong for her.

The dude with the gun kept it on me while he backed over to Jazz. When he reached her, he ripped open her blouse... she wasn't wearing a bra.

"Cut one of her tits off!" he growled, speaking English, obviously for my benefit.

One of the guys holding her pulled a switchblade from his pocket, flicked it open, and held it under her right breast ready to slice.

"Wait!" I shouted hurriedly. "Do it, and you'll get nothing from me! I'll give you what you want. Just let her go!"

The guy with the gun nodded to fatso; he took the knife away and pushed Jazz back onto the lounge. She struggled to cover herself.

"Get it!" the gunman ordered.

I held up my hands in compliance. "Okay, okay, take it easy... no-one's trying to resist you." I struggled up. "It's in the bedroom," I said with my hands raised and then slowly, cautiously, led him to my bedroom. The .38 was in the bedside drawer. I thought about it but decided against going for it for Jazz's sake. I carefully retrieved the iPod from my secret whippy and handed it over.

"There, I guess this is what you're after, the photo is on it."

"Show me!" he said, jabbing me in my already bruised ribs with the gun, and it hurt like hell. Luckily, there was enough charge for the iPod to boot up. I opened the photos folder, found the shot, and showed him.

He snatched it out of my hand, and even though I sensed it coming, I wasn't quick enough to dodge the brutal pistol whip across the jaw — out went the lights.

When I revived from that dark place, it felt like I'd been trampled by a herd of buffalo. There was hardly a part of me that wasn't aching. I clambered up from the bedroom floor and checked the time on my bedside clock; it was 6 A.M. I'd been out cold all bloody night. Jazz hadn't come in to wake me, so either she was being thoughtful or they'd kidnapped her. When I staggered out into the living room, I found the latter to be correct. There wasn't much I could do at that hour, so I went back into the bedroom and collapsed on the bed.

The sunlight streaming in the window from the living room woke me at 9:20 a.m. I dragged myself into the bathroom and took a quick shower, hoping it would revive me — it didn't.

I vaguely remembered checking earlier that Jazz wasn't on the lounge and she'd been taken. My face was too sore to shave, my ribs aching so much I couldn't even dry myself properly... but at least I was alive.

I rang Rick and filled him in. He told me to stay put and not to touch anything; he warned that the case was getting uglier by the minute.

I badly needed a coffee, so I went to the kitchen, grabbed a carton of milk from the fridge, and took a swig. It was as thick as yogurt... sour — gross, I nearly threw up. That took the edge off making coffee or breakfast, so I went down to Grind Café and had raisin toast and fresh coffee. I rang Ty and told him the bad news. It was the first time I'd heard him go off in a panic. I told him to calm down, I was on the case... Detective Malone was on his way to meet me. He kept on repeating: they will kill her, Axis... these bastards are animals. That wasn't news to me, but I understood his anguish. I finally got him off the phone as I saw through the window two cop cars pulling up outside.It felt good to be back in my flat. I immediately went to my secret whippy and retrieved Rosy's iPod. I flopped onto the lounge to work out how to get the photo of Grant Lee and Chiang off the device, so I could send it to Rick. I gave up and decided I'd better ask someone tech-savvy like Jazz. I was just about to phone her when the intercom buzzed. I answered — it was Jazz — I buzzed her up. I put the iPod back and quickly tidied up the flat. My ribs killed me with every bend; I needed a few painkillers.

A knock at the door sent me to open it. I flung it open ready to give her a big hug and copped a punch in the face. The force reeled me backwards, and I hit the floor, banging my head so hard it very nearly knocked me out. Blinking my eyes, trying to stay conscious, I peered up through the flying stars at two burly guys standing over me, their faces distorted by stockings covering their heads. They looked surreal, but the reality was that one of them had a gun pointed at my face, with the other one brandishing a baseball bat.

The guy with the gun ordered, "Get up."

I wasn't about to argue and struggled to my feet, holding my throbbing jaw. Another guy pushed Jazz ahead of him through the door. The three of them were Chinese. I'm sure one of them was the big guy that whacked me in the office a week ago.

The guy holding Jazz savagely pushed her onto the lounge, then barked at her in Cantonese, I guess to stay put, while he viciously gagged her. Her face looked pale, panicked, her normally neat and tidy appearance all roughed up. But to her credit, she wasn't whimpering. To the contrary, she had a look in her eye that given half the chance, she'd rip her attacker's head off. We exchanged a glance, and her eyes softened for me.

Whack! A pistol smacked me in the temple and sent my head reeling.

"Where is the photo?" The guy who'd whacked me demanded through clenched teeth with a heavily accented voice.

"What photo!" I snapped back at him, as a tepid rivulet of blood trickled down my cheek from a cut in my head.

"Okay, have it your way, Gweilo! Hold her!" he aggressively ordered, and the two guys grabbed Jazz by the arms.

He commanded angrily, "Lift her!"

They rough-handled her to her feet. She struggled against their grip, but there was no point; they were too strong for her.

The dude with the gun kept it on me while he backed over to Jazz. When he reached her, he ripped open her blouse... she wasn't wearing a bra.

"Cut one of her tits off!" he growled, speaking English, obviously for my benefit.

One of the guys holding her pulled a switchblade from his pocket, flicked it open, and held it under her right breast ready to slice.

"Wait!" I shouted hurriedly. "Do it, and you'll get nothing from me! I'll give you what you want. Just let her go!"

The guy with the gun nodded to fatso; he took the knife away and pushed Jazz back onto the lounge. She struggled to cover herself.

"Get it!" the gunman ordered.

I held up my hands in compliance. "Okay, okay, take it easy... no-one's trying to resist you." I struggled up. "It's in the bedroom," I said with my hands raised and then slowly, cautiously, led him to my bedroom. The .38 was in the bedside drawer. I thought about it but decided against going for it for Jazz's sake. I carefully retrieved the iPod from my secret whippy and handed it over.

"There, I guess this is what you're after, the photo is on it."

"Show me!" he said, jabbing me in my already bruised ribs with the gun, and it hurt like hell. Luckily, there was enough charge for the iPod to boot up. I opened the photos folder, found the shot, and showed him.

He snatched it out of my hand, and even though I sensed it coming, I wasn't quick enough to dodge the brutal pistol whip across the jaw — out went the lights.

When I revived from that dark place, it felt like I'd been trampled by a herd of buffalo. There was hardly a part of me that wasn't aching. I clambered up from the bedroom floor and checked the time on my bedside clock; it was 6 A.M. I'd been out cold all bloody night. Jazz hadn't come in to wake me, so either she was being thoughtful or they'd kidnapped her. When I staggered out into the living room, I found the latter to be correct. There wasn't much I could do at that hour, so I went back into the bedroom and collapsed on the bed.

The sunlight streaming in the window from the living room woke me at 9:20 a.m. I dragged myself into the bathroom and took a quick shower, hoping it would revive me — it didn't.

I vaguely remembered checking earlier that Jazz wasn't on the lounge and she'd been taken. My face was too sore to shave, my ribs aching so much I couldn't even dry myself properly... but at least I was alive.

I rang Rick and filled him in. He told me to stay put and not to touch anything; he warned that the case was getting uglier by the minute.

I badly needed a coffee, so I went to the kitchen, grabbed a carton of milk from the fridge, and took a swig. It was as thick as yogurt... sour — gross, I nearly threw up. That took the edge off making coffee or breakfast, so I went down to Grind Café and had raisin toast and fresh coffee. I rang Ty and told him the bad news. It was the first time I'd heard him go off in a panic. I told him to calm down, I was on the case... Detective Malone was on his way to meet me. He kept on repeating: they will kill her, Axis... these bastards are animals. That wasn't news to me, but I understood his anguish. I finally got him off the phone as I saw through the window two cop cars pulling up outside.

CHAPTER EIGHTEEN

I WENT OUT front of the café to catch Rick.

"Bloody hell!" he growled with a snigger. "You look like crap!"

"Yeah, well imagine how I feel inside," I rasped.

"Go back into the café and order me a black coffee while I send uniforms up to dust your flat. Give me your keycard."

I handed it over and went back into the café to order.

After a while, Rick came in and sat down.

"Pretty rugged case this one, old son," he announced before I had time to open my mouth.

"Yeah, my fee will go in cosmetic surgery if this keeps up."

"Did you get a look at them?"

"There were three of 'em ... Chinese, wearing brown stockings over their heads. I reckon one of them was the same guy that clubbed me at the office last week. But I'd never pick them from mug shots, if that's what you mean, unless they're all wearing stockings in the photos."

"Glad you still have your sense of humour," he said with a friendly smile.

"Well, you've gotta laugh, as my Dad used to say. How did they get Jazz with a police guard on her?" I said seriously.

"I've sent DI Parker to her apartment to determine that."

"So, what does this do for our case against Grant Lee?"

"Without evidence, we have no case."

"Mate," I grinned at him. "Are you kidding me? I'm walking evidence."

I knew he was spot on, but that didn't make me feel any better. It was blatantly obvious who was behind it all and the two murders, but right now, we couldn't prove a damn thing.

"Has Bill been able to turn up anything on him?" I prodded.

"No, the bastard is as clean as a whistle. Too bloody clean, not that it means anything."

"Is he still doing his job?"

"Yeah, but we've got eyes and ears all over him. We even got his cellphone records but found nothing — he must have a specific phone for calling his brother and gang members."

His phone rang. "Malone ... yes, figured as much. Okay, have 'em dust the place ... don't suppose he got a look at them? Yeah, just like Axis. Okay, see you back at HQ." He put his phone on the table. "That was Parker, she found the guard inside the apartment hogtied and gagged ... No ID on them, they had stockings over their faces."

"What about CCTV in the street?"

"That's Harry's gig, he's onto it, never know might get a number plate, but you can back it out it'd be stolen. Triads are smooth operators, Axis. They rarely leave a clue ... but we still have to go through the rigors."

"Maybe DI Zhong in Hong Kong can get the cellphone records of the brother's calls. They wouldn't be expecting that."

"Good idea, I'll give him a bell. A good bloke?"

"Saved my life," I said with a sigh.

~ ~ ~

Later in my office, I was lazing back with my feet up on the desk, doodling on a notepad racking my brain for clues when "Someday Soon" chimed in. I answered, "Stone ... Oh, g'day Ty, you have?" I sat up sharply when he said he'd heard from the kidnappers. "Really, okay ... I'll get onto Malone ... no, we have to ... what? Listen, after all I've been through, that's asking too much ... All right, all right ... I know what comes with the job. It is my business, isn't it?" I growled. "You're where? Okay, I'll come there now." After I finished the call, I immediately rang Rick. "Hi, just got a call from Ty Sun. He's heard from the kidnappers. They want a signed deal for a majority share in the Golden Dragon and two hundred grand in cash ... No, they specifically said no cops or Jazz dies ... he bloody-well wants me to do the exchange. Mate, even if I was feeling my best, I'd be nervous about that ... No, he wants me to meet him at the Golden Dragon now ... Where's Grant Lee? In his office ... hmm, okay, Zhong's onto it, oh, good ... okay, see you there."

I hung up. At least Zhong was able to access Lee's phone records in Hong Kong. I was hoping it would show Grant Lee's secret Sydney number, so we could get his phone log here.

~ ~ ~

The sunny day lifted my spirits somewhat during the short walk to the Golden Dragon on nearby Dixon Street. The receptionist greeted me with a big, buck-toothed smile and directed me to the back room. I joined Rick and Ty at the table.

"Gentlemen, anything new?" I asked urgently.

"Yes, we lifted prints from Miss Sun's apartment and yours," Rick explained. "When Parker ran them through AFIS, she got a match: Fang Peng Jian. He has a criminal record, did two years for possession of an unlicensed firearm."

"Have you heard of him, Ty?" I asked.

"No," he replied gruffly.

"I've sent officers with Parker to his apartment in Newtown. She has a warrant under the terrorism act."

"Handy," I observed.

"Yeah, one good thing that came out of all the crap in the Middle East, Ukraine, and with COVID is that we don't have to waste time anymore getting warrants," Rick remarked.

"How are we going to get my daughter back?" Ty snapped impatiently.

"You give Axis two hundred grand, he sets up the exchange, and we grab them," Rick said emphatically.

"But as soon as they sense cops, they'll kill her. That's for certain," Ty growled furiously, then glared at me.

"They won't know what hit them. I plan on using our friend Lee Kit Wo, also known as Detective Sergeant Grant Lee, to set it up," Rick said.

"How will you do that?" I asked.

"He has no idea that we're onto him. If we can get his phone number from Hong Kong," he held up crossed fingers, "we can give him the opportunity to join his mates, and then track his phone to lead us to them."

"You're depending on someone in Hong Kong to get his number?" Ty said, lacking confidence in his tone.

"It's all we've got, Ty. Unless you have a better plan?" I asked.

"No, the only alternative is to give them what they want and deal with it later," Ty said.

"You'd be risking Jazz and Axis' lives if you do that. Besides, what makes you think they won't just keep asking for more?" Rick posed.

"My bet is that the two hundred grand is something they've come up with here, as it wasn't part of the deal we made in Hong Kong. They want two million, but that's after the share transfer," I explained.

"Sounds plausible, Axis. Besides, two hundred grand isn't enough money for a kidnapping," Rick added.

"Do you think the Lee brothers are not in agreement?" Ty asked me.

"Not sure. It's possible that the kidnappers are after the money, and Grant Lee might not even know they've asked for it," I suggested.

"Remember, he's under watch in his office at police HQ. For all intents and purposes, he might have ordered documents to be exchanged, knowing that the two million comes next," Rick considered.

"If we assume that, then we must also assume discord among their ranks. That's why this could be an even more dangerous situation than Grant Lee thinks it is," Ty summarised.

"Exactly," Rick said.

"I'll tell you what, if the exchange is on a bloody boat, I'm not doing it," I complained.

"Why? What do you have against boats?" Ty asked.

"Plenty," I grumbled.

"Where are you with the share certificate, Mr Sun?" Rick asked.

"My accountant is at ASIC, getting the transfer notarised."

"And the money?" I questioned.

"The HSBC will deliver it here soon. Then what happens?" Ty asked.

"We're banking on Zhong getting back to us with Lee's number. Then we can put things in place to locate the kidnappers," Rick said.

"It's a gamble then?" Ty observed.

"Kidnapping always is. Axis knows that, don't you?" Rick agreed.

I figured Ty liked the idea of it being a gamble. Punters are like that. As for me, I try not to gamble on anything, not even a lottery ticket. It's a mug's game. Any money I earn comes from putting my neck on the line, so I'm not about to give it away cheaply, especially to bloody bookies. I've had too many customers in the racing game for me to believe any sport is honest anymore. It was okay when I was growing up. Athletes played sports for pride... the horses were as rigged then, and there were far fewer sports enhancement drugs. But now, the internet has provided a world of opportunities for folks to punt. You can bet on two people peeing up a wall anywhere in the world, online. Gambling has corrupted sports in my book, and that's just another one of those things in life that really ticks me off.

Rick's phone rang. It was Parker... someone was at Fang's Newtown apartment. She wanted permission to go in. But Rick wasn't ready. He ordered a continued stakeout until he had everything in order. We were playing the waiting game, and it was nerve-racking.

My stomach began to growl, craving food, when Rick's phone rang again. This time it was Zhong, and we were in luck. Lee Kok Lung's phone records showed twenty numbers in Sydney, and he made a daily call to one of them. Zhong had emailed the entire phone log to Rick. Our spirits were lifted, things were starting to go our way. Rick phoned Parker and instructed her to check the numbers with the telecommunications company. Although it was likely that Grant would be using a prepaid SIM card to avoid detection, it was still worth a try.

"We have to decide whether to roll the dice on this number that your Dragon Head buddy in Hong Kong frequently calls, belonging to Grant Lee. We have no way to confirm it. Our entire plan will be riding on that phone number. So, it's up to you, Mr Sun," Rick proposed.

"Tell me the last three digits of the phone number," he asked.

"Triple four," Rick replied with a frown.

"Four is a Triad number from ancient times. It signifies the member's position in the organisation and the four oceans that surround China and, ultimately, the universe," Ty explained.

"What do you mean by the member's position?" I queried.

"A Dragon Head is triple four," he said with a wry smile.

"We've got him!" Rick said excitedly. "Now, we put phase one of the operation in motion."

CHAPTER NINETEEN

RICK PHONED PARKER and instructed her to place a GPS tracker on the number we believed to be Grant Lee's. Then, he called Bill Rogers at vice and asked him to give Grant Lee a couple of days off work, making the excuse plausible. The trap was set. All we needed was for the kidnappers to call Ty with the exchange details, and for Grant to pay his mates a visit.

One of Ty's bodyguards entered and conveyed something to him in Cantonese. Ty gave him an order, which sent him back outside.

He glared at us and ruefully announced, "The money has arrived."

The big guy returned with a briefcase, handed it to Ty, and left. Ty placed it on the table and opened it. The money was neatly stacked in twenty ten-thousand-dollar bundles. Ty read a note left inside the case by the HSBC branch manager.

"The bag has a concealed GPS, and some of the notes have microdot locators," he said, then picked up a cellphone from the briefcase. "The phone is equipped with a tracking app for the briefcase and the notes."

"Very professional," Rick remarked.

Ty handed me the cellphone and locked the case. I booted it up and opened the app, which showed the bag and the money as stationary at the Golden Dragon Restaurant. It even displayed a schematic of the building, indicating the precise location of the items within.

"How's that?" I said, showing Rick.

"Clever, very clever indeed," he acknowledged. "I need to get back to the office to coordinate the stakeout in Newtown. Do you need me for anything else here?"

"No, once we receive the call, I'll let you know, and we can work out an exchange strategy," I proposed.

Ty sighed deeply. "Why haven't they called?"

"You'll have to be patient, Mr Sun," Rick said. "It'll happen. Axis is experienced with abductions. He did a great job solving one in the Philippines just a month ago."

"Let's just relax and have something to eat," I suggested.

"Okay, talk to you when you have something. Catch you later," Rick said, oozing confidence.

As soon as Rick closed the door behind him, Ty spoke his mind.

"I have never been one to trust the police. That's why I hired you, Axis. And now, it seems we are in their hands."

"If your daughter hadn't been kidnapped, we wouldn't be in this situation, Ty," I countered.

"If the police had done their job in the first place, she wouldn't have been abducted... Ah? I rest my case."

"I guess you're right," I said with a shrug. "But you have to agree we have no other option, not if you care about Jazz—"

"That goes without saying, but I'm not sure I'm willing to risk her life on a gamble that the police will be successful. They have nothing to lose, you see, unlike you and me... Did the police solve your kidnapping in the Philippines?"

"No, but I utilised their help when necessary."

"Ah, now we're getting somewhere."

During lunch, we discussed the possible outcomes of the kidnapping and identified the best course of action.

A little while later, Ty's phone rang. We sprang into action, thinking it might be the kidnappers, but no. Judging by his mood swing and the fact that he was speaking English, I could tell it was someone else.

When he finished the call, he said, "That was my accountant. The share certificate transfers are official. Fifty-one percent of the equity in the Golden Dragon now belongs to Lee Kok Lung. Once he has a copy of the certificate, he can call an extraordinary meeting of the board of directors at his leisure. Since he holds the majority vote, he can appoint a new CEO to replace me. I will then be demoted to managing director."

"Because you're the only other director, does that mean he has two votes?" I asked.

"That is correct."

"You know, I had the opportunity to rectify this months ago and didn't," he admitted.

"How so?"

"A few months ago, Chiang got involved in something... I might as well be honest with you, he was involved in drug trafficking. You know that because you saw the photo of him with Grant Lee and the drugs. Well, that was only half of it. First of all, Rosy was my plant."

"What?" The revelation stunned me.

"Her family owed me for giving her a job at the restaurant. Chiang was interested in her, so I used her to spy on him... just to keep track of what he was doing, mind you... He wouldn't tell me anything about his activities, you understand... a loose cannon."

"Wait a second, so Rosy took that photo for you? What were you planning to do with it?" I asked carefully.

"I was planning to blackmail whoever Chiang was dealing with at Sun Yee On, in exchange for dropping my gambling debt. As it turned out, I heard that the guy in the photo was a cop, so I abandoned the idea... I never even laid eyes on the photo. Rosy just told me she had it."

"So, put down Rosy in front of Jazz because she was undercover for you?"

"That is correct. I regret that she had to die, and in such a terrible manner," he shook his head shamefully.

"If you had spoken up earlier, we might have saved her life," I snapped angrily.

"Yes, you're right, I know. But sometimes, less said is better."

I took a deep breath to stop myself from hitting him. "Not when people are risking their lives for you, Ty," I growled scornfully.

"Yes, yes, you're right."

"I don't care what nationality you are. It's all about trust... and now I think you should learn to—" "Someday Soon" interrupted me. I took the call.

"Hey Rick, what's up? Yeah, I'm thinking of wrapping things up here as well... We can all stay on alert by phone. You will? Okay, that's good. Later," I hung up.

"Rick said the stakeout in Newtown will continue overnight... and that Grant Lee had left the office and gone to his Maroubra Beach apartment. He's still there. DS Parker will monitor Lee twenty-four-seven. Rick has a meeting with the Commissioner of Police now and will go home after that... He'll only be a phone call away. I think I might do a couple of things and then head home myself," I said, standing a little despondent.

Ty extended a tentative hand to shake. "I do trust you, Axis, as much as I trust Nick. And you know I trust him like a brother."

He pulled me into an embrace, and it was the first true display of emotion I had witnessed from him.

"Okay, call me as soon as you hear from them. I'll only be ten minutes away. Don't worry, Ty. This will turn out positively. Keep an eye on that briefcase."

"Thank you, Axis."

I sensed a hint of tears welling up in his tired eyes.

~ ~ ~

What I needed most was to stock up on food. The cupboard was bare. The nearest supermarket was Woolworths at Haymarket, just a few minutes' walk from the restaurant.

It was peak hour, but I didn't mind navigating the sidewalk amidst hurried pedestrians.

I had forgotten about my ribs, and by the time I reached my apartment with all the shopping bags, I was in agony. It took a couple of painkillers and three fingers of neat JD to ease the pain. Free from discomfort, I turned on the TV and watched the news. "Someday Soon" roused me from a deep sleep. It was Nick... I muted the TV and put him on speaker.

"Hey, buddy, how's it going?"

"Good, how are your aches and pains?"

"Ah, they're improving."

"Ty just called and filled me in. It's good that Zhong got the number..."

"Yeah, let's hope it's the right one. We have a lot riding on it."

"Do you think the old man is handling it?" Nick inquired.

"Yeah, he's one tough old goat... I was worried about him at first, but he's a realist. It sounds hypocritical, but he's also a smart punter."

"I don't know, Axis. He did rack up a hefty gambling debt, so he might not be that smart."

"I hear you... well, we'll have to take a chance on this one. But you know, I just don't get why guys as clued up as these Triads would be asking for two hundred grand in cash along with the share certificate. They must know the notes would be marked, wouldn't they?"

"Ty said you think the kidnappers are working independently of Grant Lee. That might explain it. They're probably in it for a quick buck and haven't thought it through. There'll be hell to pay once the Dragon Head finds out."

"Yeah, it'll be interesting to see how that plays out."

"Don't expect it to. I reckon he'll find out and change the ransom. That might be why it's taking so long for them to get back with the exchange details."

"Old territory, mate," I said with a chuckle. "I hope it doesn't turn out like the last one, with the demand not being paid and all hell breaking loose."

"Are you ever going to let me live that one down?"

"Probably not," I joked.

"Here, someone wants to speak to you—"

There was a rustle as he handed the phone to someone.

"Hello, stranger..." a soft female voice purred.

I immediately recognised it.

"Well, if it isn't my lovely suicide blonde... How are you, Lola? I bet you really miss me?"

"Only when I'm in bed."

"Oh shucks, I bet you say that to all the fellas," I teased.

"When are you coming up to see me?"

"I'll be there as soon as I've got this case boxed, I promise."

I immediately thought of Suzie waiting for me at Nick's place in Manila, and Jazz with her lovely legs and feet. Boy, I was in demand, or so I kidded myself.

"Okay, I'll hold you to your promise, Mr Happy. You be good now and don't go getting hurt."

I thought, if only she knew the state I was in.

"Okay, baby, kiss, kiss..."

"Bye for now, sweetie."

There was another rustle, and Nick came back on the line. "I think she misses you, mate."

"Her and the rest... I'll call you once I've got this done."

"Good luck. Are you sure you can handle this without me, Kemosabe?"

"Yes, Tonto, but for now, it's... Hi-Yo Silver, away!"

~ ~ ~

"Someday Soon" woke me up at 7 a.m. It was Ty. The kidnappers had made contact at 6 a.m. with a time and specific instructions. I agreed to meet Ty at my office at 8:30 to talk it through.

Feeling revitalised after a good night's sleep, I stopped by The Grind Café and grabbed a coffee to go. Bathed in sunlight, I confidently walked to my office building and took the elevator up.

Sitting behind my desk, I decided to start the day by lacing my coffee with a shot of bourbon. I quickly downed it, and that got things going. If I had used whiskey, it would be called an Irish coffee, but with bourbon, I wondered: is it a Kentucky Coffee?

Realising that I hadn't checked my email since starting the case, I powered up my Mac. Just as I did, there was a knock on the door. I opened it to find Ty standing there.

"Are you alright?" I asked. "You look flustered... Pull up a chair."

"I haven't slept, Axis. I need a drink," he gasped.

I poured him a shot of bourbon and handed it to him.

He took a sip and grimaced. "Yuck, what is that?"

"Bourbon, sorry. It's all I've got... It's an acquired taste, I suppose."

He still downed it and then held out his glass for another. I obliged.

"So, tell me what he said?" I asked.

"They changed the demand... I guess it was like you and DI Malone thought. When the Dragon Head found out they asked for cash, he reacted... So now they're asking for 2 million to be paid into an account they'll specify. Once they have the money and the share certificate, they'll return Jazz."

"Figured as much. Right, so the first thing we need to do is call Rick, inform him about the change of plans, and get an update on Grant Lee's movements overnight, as well as the results of the stakeout."

CHAPTER TWENTY

THE JD HAD brought colour back to Ty's face. He nodded for me to continue and I called Rick.

Rick was in the middle of plotting Grant Lee's movements on his office murder board. He asked both of us to come to his office to talk, but Ty refused, fearing that being seen could cause more problems for Jazz. Rick agreed and said he would get a printout of the murder board and come to my office.

We didn't have to wait long before Rick and Parker arrived. After introducing DS Jess Parker to Ty, we sat around the coffee table, examining the printout of Grant Lee's movements tracked by his cellphone.

Rick explained, "We're glad it's the right phone number. Checking his address confirmed that. He left the office at 1:30 and went directly to his Maroubra Beach apartment."

Parker provided background information. "Lee lives alone in a three-bedroom penthouse apartment on Marine Parade, Maroubra Beach."

Rick continued, "At 7:30 p.m., he left his apartment and went to the Fortune Garden Restaurant. Then, at 9 p.m., he drove to an office block on Thomas Street, Ultimo, which we believe to be his office or the offices of Sun Yee On. From there, he made three phone calls. The first one was to a silent number, probably a pre-paid, which we couldn't triangulate due to limited call time. The second call was international to Hong Kong, a number we identified as belonging to his brother Lee Kok Lung. And the third call was to the same pre-paid number, which we managed to triangulate to the general area of Huntley Street, Alexandria. Based on what we know now, this is likely the location of the kidnappers."

Jess took over. "He found out that they had asked for cash, called his brother, and then called the kidnappers back with a changed plan."

Ty asked, "What time was the last call made?"

Jess checked her records. "05:17."

"I received the call from them at 6 a.m., so it adds up, doesn't it?" Ty said.

"Sure does," I agreed enthusiastically. "And the stakeout?"

"No one has entered or exited the Newtown apartment. This tells us that Fang Peng Jian hasn't been home," Jess said.

Rick asked, "What are the new demands, Mr Sun?"

"They want 2 million to be sent to a specified account, along with the executed share transfer certificate. They'll text the account number at midday. Once the money is in the account, I'll receive the final instructions for Jazz's safe return," Ty explained.

"Do you have that kind of money, Mr Sun?" Jess inquired.

"No, I don't," Ty replied.

"Can you arrange for it?" Rick asked.

"Yes, the bank will loan it to me against the Golden Dragon, but with the shares having been transferred, there might be some complications," Ty said.

"Please find out, Ty. Give your accountant a call," I suggested.

He nodded and moved away to make the call in private.

"You realise that once he makes the transfer, the money is gone, and he won't be able to get it back?" I mentioned. "I went through a similar scenario during the Kitty Lovejoy kidnapping in Manila."

"Well, it comes down to whether Mr Sun is prepared to risk his daughter's life by going in with guns blazing or not," Rick said slowly.

"It's not like he doesn't owe the money; it is a gambling debt, isn't it?" Jess observed.

"Yes, it is. He'll need something from the Fortune Garden to confirm the debt has been cleared," I added.

"They won't do that. It would make them complicit in the kidnapping," Rick stated.

Ty returned and sat down. He appeared distressed, and after a short time, he spoke abruptly, "It can be done, but it will mean mortgaging my home, business, and Jazz's apartment."

I could see the anguish in his eyes, but Parker was right. He had gotten himself into this situation, owing the money. The illegal part was the crooks using extortion to get it back.

"Okay, here's the plan. Ty will pay the money once he receives the account number. Then, when they call with the drop-off location, I'll take the original share transfer certificate to exchange it for Jazz. Rick, can you work with that?"

"We'll need to get Grant Lee to the location or physically make the exchange; otherwise, we'll only be able to arrest the kidnappers," Rick explained.

"He's unlikely to put himself in that position now that he has the only evidence, the photo," I said.

"But what about when he ultimately takes a seat on the Golden Dragon board? Wouldn't that be enough to arrest him?" Ty questioned.

"I'm afraid not, Ty," Rick outlined. "By sending the money offshore, we won't have anything directly tying it to him. As for the share certificate, it's in his brother's name, and I expect Grant will be appointed as CEO. There's nothing illegal about that. No, the only way we can get him is in direct relation to the kidnapping."

"Damn, losing that photo... We had the bastard!" I growled.

"What if Ty insists that the exchange must involve the Dragon Head?" Parker suggested.

"No, that wouldn't work," I said.

"No, wait a minute. She might have something there," Ty asserted. "What if I needed the Dragon Head to sign a receipt for the share certificate and the debt?"

"You know, that might be worth a try," I said, smiling at Parker, acknowledging her idea.

Rick stood up, and Parker followed suit. "Okay, we'll wait to hear from you next."

"Will you keep an eye on the Newtown apartment?" I asked.

"Yes," Rick confirmed, "and Grant's movements. I'll put a SWAT team on standby for the handover."

After they left, Ty looked at me sternly and said, "Axis, I don't want a SWAT team going in. It's too big of a risk."

"Okay, let's make that decision once we have the location."

~ ~ ~

I walked with Ty to the Golden Dragon, and when we arrived, he invited me inside for Yum Cha, which I gladly accepted. Dim sum had grown on me. The restaurant was bustling with customers, and as we navigated through the busy waiters, I noticed a familiar face among the diners. Initially, I brushed it off and continued to the private room.

While Ty was placing the order, a realisation suddenly hit me, causing me to jump up and startle him. Concerned, he asked me what was wrong.

"I just realised who's sitting outside in your restaurant," I exclaimed.

"Who?" he inquired.

"It's bloody Fatty Tung, the Sun Yee On enforcer, the red pole. He should be in jail!" I exclaimed.

"That can't be just a coincidence. Where are you going?" he asked as I walked away.

"I'm going to confront him," I replied.

"Be careful," he yelled after me, uttering something in Cantonese.

As I walked out into the restaurant, I noticed Ty's henchmen following me. I approached Tung and glared down at him.

"Well, look who the cat dragged in. It's Mr Red Pole, Fatty enforcer Tung. Tell me," I sarcastically leaned on the back of his chair, "what brings you to Sydney? Wait, even more importantly, how the hell did you get out of jail in Hong Kong?"

I said it loud enough for his associates to hear, in case they were unaware. Tung looked up at me, his expression turning into a scowl. He glared at me, and I noticed his change in demeanour when he spotted the bookends behind me.

"Stone, you are a very irritating person... has anyone ever told you that?" he snarled.

"Plenty, especially when they're being carted off to jail," I caustically replied.

"Can't a man travel to Sydney for business without some two-bit Aussie PI sticking his nose where it doesn't belong?" he countered.

"We'll see about that, Tung. I know what you're up to here. I warn you... don't get in my way. This isn't Hong Kong... you're on my turf now."

I gave him a death stare and didn't pay him the courtesy of a reply. I turned on my heel, signalling my escorts to walk me back to the private room. Once seated opposite Ty, he spoke uneasily.

"Tung being here isn't a good sign. Do you know what the Red Pole does in the organisation?"

"No, but you're going to tell me," I replied.

"The Dragon Head sets the policy, and the Red Pole enforces it, without question," Ty explained.

"That suggests Soy was overstepping his role as White Paper Fan by wanting to kill me. Shouldn't that have been Tung's job?" I pondered.

"Yes, although not necessarily him doing it personally, but he would have organised the hit. Soy must have had significant reasons to want you dead," Ty replied.

I knew the reason, but I had no intention of disclosing to Ty that I'd had a scene with Soy's girlfriend. There were more pressing matters at hand.

"Tung's presence raises questions: What is he here for? Is he involved in the kidnapping handover, or is he here as the Dragon

Head's eyes and ears because he doesn't trust his younger brother?" I contemplated.

"Those are good questions. I suspect the latter is the reason for his presence. I imagine Grant Lee would try to complete the task without interference from Hong Kong. Pride often drives the actions of Chinese people," Ty reasoned.

"That makes perfect sense, Ty."

"I hope you didn't challenge Tung in front of his associates. Chinese people abhor losing face and will feel compelled to retaliate out of pride," Ty warned.

"Hmm, there might be a bit of an issue there," I admitted.

When I left the restaurant, Tung was nowhere to be seen. I decided to head to my office but received a call just as I entered the building. I stopped and answered, "Stone, who's calling?"

"You don't need to know my name, but I can tell you this... he is here to kill you. You know who I'm talking about," a soft voice on the other end warned.

"The Red Pole?" I guessed.

"I can say no more. I'm just warning you. Goodbye, Mr Stone. Good luck."

The call ended, and there was no number displayed. The voice sounded Asian but had an Aussie accent. Who could it be, and why would they warn me? Regardless, I needed to stay vigilant.

I decided against going up to the office, knowing I had been caught there before. Since I had left my .38 at home, I felt more at ease having it with me, so I headed there instead. On the way, I called Rick and informed him about Fatty Tung being in town and the warning I had received. He believed the two were connected. I asked if Grant Lee had made any additional movements, such as heading to the airport to meet Tung. However, Rick informed me that Grant had remained at his apartment all morning and hadn't made any further calls from his disposable phone. I suggested he check the arrival manifests and immigration records of flights from Hong Kong over the past 24 hours to identify Tung's entry. Once Tung was identified, Rick planned to review the CCTV footage to see who had met him. I let Rick proceed with the investigation and ended the call.

~ ~ ~

Sitting on the couch with my pistol cleaning kit on my lap, I poured myself a neat JD to ease the pain. It was my preferred medicine. As I prepared to clean my .38, I decided to put on some music for background ambiance. I grabbed the remote and triggered the CD player, not knowing which album was loaded. To my surprise, Pink Floyd's Division Bell began playing, starting with the track "Cluster One." The music matched the mood of the moment, but as the second track, "What Do You Want from Me," started playing, the lyrics felt personal. The words echoed the threat from Fatty Tung: "Do you want my blood—what do you want?" It was all in my mind, of course, but I've always had a thing about omens.

I recalled an encounter I had years ago with a girl named Vanessa, who turned out to be a practicing witch. After a passionate one-night stand, she warned me not to drive on a specific day. Although I initially dismissed it, I ended up in a severe car accident on that very day in Sydney. It could have been fatal, but perhaps because I was subconsciously prepared for it, I survived. Vanessa had taught me to listen to my conscience and pay attention to omens. Call me old-fashioned, but I've always believed that denying superstition is, in itself, a form of superstition. With that in mind, I decided to turn off the CD player before any more lyrics could affect my thoughts.

CHAPTER TWENTY-ONE

"NOT ANOTHER KIDNAPPING!" beautiful Lola screamed.

I woke with a jolt, holding the barrel of my .38—I must have nodded off. "What a dream I'd been having... I badly needed another JD."

It was quarter to six and getting dark. I turned on the lights and poured myself a JD. It wasn't like me to sleep during the day... sleeping in during the morning, sure. I was a night owl, and it came with the territory—though my mother always said that because I was born at 4 A.M., I was a night person condemned to the realm of vampires, sinister nightlife, and the pool halls of life forever."

The evening dragged on. I cooked steak, eggs, and fries for dinner... polished off a few more JDs and watched a dubbed movie on Netflix that was about as memorable as a photograph of a toothbrush. Close to midnight, I was tempted to ring Ty. I knew he'd be up but decided against it. It would all have to wait until tomorrow. With my companion parked within reach, I curled up in bed with a book.

A protesting bladder woke me at 7 A.M. I'd had enough sleep for a month anyway, so I put on the TV and made a pot of coffee and a round of toast with Promite.

By half past eight, I was all spruced up and ready to go when "Someday Soon" kick-started the day.

"'Stone... Hey Rick, what's doing?'"

"'I need you in here.'"

He had his grumpy voice on.

"'What's the problem? You don't sound too friendly.'"

"'Do I always have to sound friendly, Axis?' he grated."

"'No, I guess not... it was just an observation.'"

"'Look, I've spent the last hour being hauled over the coals by the boss, now he wants to speak to you.'"

"'Oh, crap. Nothing worse than Humpty Dumpty wanting to stick his bib into a case I'm on. You know how much he hates me... or should I say every bloody PI in the business,' I snarled."

"'Yes, I know Donald is intolerant of PIs, but unfortunately, this time, he's got a case.'"

"'Fill me in.'"

"'No, he'll do that better than I. Come down to my office once you've been upstairs. He's expecting you at 9.30.'"

"'All right, I'll hit the frog and toad now, catch you there,'" I signed off. Superintendent Humphrey Donald, whom I'd nicknamed Humpty Dumpty because he was half the size of a bus, couldn't stand the sight of me. We had a history of face-offs over the last ten years, and I wasn't looking forward to this one. Normally, I could count on Rick for support, but it seemed that wasn't going to be the case this round. I decided to change into something more suitable for the meeting, so I dusted down my only grey suit, dug out my only necktie, unearthed a nearly clean white shirt, and decked myself out. I even found my old leather briefcase under a pile of Playboy magazines, so I rubbed the mildew off it and then cruised downstairs, feeling pretty good about myself. It didn't take long to catch a cab to police HQ in Surry Hills.

~ ~ ~

I checked my reflection in the closed polished steel elevator doors on my way up to the headmaster's office. That's how it felt: I'd been summoned.

I entered his domain and faced his haggard secretary. "Good morning, Miss Carpin, I'm here to see the Superintendent."

"Take a seat, Mr. Stone, he will see you when he's ready," she said as dull as dishwater.

"Where would you like me to take it," I joked just to needle her. She just stared blankly at me. I sat down and mumbled under my breath just loud enough for her to hear, "Well, some people have a sense of humour."

I'd counted the carpet tiles on the floor, read Women's Weekly, and picked all the lint off the front of my suit jacket by the time I was ushered into his lordship's office.

I sat in the sole chair positioned in front of his desk and waited for the huge double-chinned lump of a man to look up from what he was reading to acknowledge my existence. When it didn't happen, I decided to speak up.

"Good morning, sir!" I'd figured to raise my voice a little above the normal, so he'd have no chance of pretending he didn't hear me. Only somewhere along the way, I made a miscalculation, and my voice erupted into the room in one great volcanic blast of sound that could have awakened the dead. But it got the desired result; he looked up and over his small round wire frame glasses, and scowled at me.

"Stone," he grumbled distastefully, like he'd bitten into a lemon. He peeled off his glasses for added impact and held up the paper he'd been reading. "This is a report of the Sun kidnapping signed off by Inspector Malone, it doesn't mention you... until the most important part, the handover, which Malone is under the delusion you are in control of... So, I ask myself, when I go to the commissioner to explain why we've laid off an officer, Detective Grant Lee, held a twenty-four-seven stakeout on a Newtown apartment, spent a fortune on technology surveillance—do I tell him it was all for Axis Stone, so he could get paid his fat fee?"

"Oh, I think there's a little more to it than that, superintendent," I countered. "You wouldn't have a case if I hadn't brought it to you. Your department was wading around with sharks in a pond studying a dead leg without a clue until I cracked the case open for you... so is this what I get in thanks, some sort of schoolboy dressing down from you?"

"Your impertinence is legendary, Stone. I remind you it is your duty as a citizen to bring the police information of a crime that might lead to a conviction!"

"I am a licensed private detective, Superintendent Donald, and that license gives me the right to operate within the law and act for clients who aren't being satisfied by the police system."

There's no ham like a big ham. The Superintendent proved it with the most elaborate double take I've seen in ages. And then he exploded.

"Don't you read the letter of the law to me, boy!"

"Look, sir, you can build your blood pressure up another five points by bawling me out, but that isn't going to get us anywhere. I act for Mr Ty Sun. It is his daughter that has been kidnapped. It is my job to get her back safely, and I am working with your office to facilitate such. If you don't like it, then that's your problem. To be frank, we have bigger problems than that on our hands, and all this crap is just slowing us down... Now, ask me a question and I'll give you an answer, and if that helps you with the Commissioner, then good. But let me make this perfectly clear—nothing is going to distract me from doing my job on this case."

"Be that as it may, Stone, you will tow-the-line with the police. I understand it is on your say-so that DI Malone has had DI Bill Rogers lay off DS Lee, but when I asked for a reason, none, none, was forthcoming."

"So, is that what this is all about? Why didn't you just say that in the first place?" I said stiffly.

I realised the problem, and it was a sticky one. Rick obviously hadn't told Humpty of our suspicion that Lee was the local Dragon Head of the Sun Yee On. He couldn't run the risk. I had to think of what to say to settle the situation. Rick must be hoping for me to save the day. I had an idea.

"Look, I was in Hong Kong a few days ago, working with the Hong Kong police in connection to the possible involvement of a Triad organised crime ring called the Sun Yee On in this case. After a meeting with the leaders of the Sun Yee On, one of them tried to shoot me and was shot and killed by the police. The leader is Lee Kok Lung, who we believe to be the older brother of DS Grant Lee. That being the case, to avoid a conflict of interest, it was decided by your people to keep this confidential and have DS Grant Lee kept clear of the case until the allegation can be substantiated. Does that make sense?"

There was a long pause while he digested all of that.

"I suppose it does," he said in a derisive tone.

I'd beaten him and couldn't help but smile. "Will there be anything else, sir?"

"No, thank you for coming in, Stone," he said expressionlessly. He put his glasses back on and returned to looking down at his paperwork. I'd been dismissed.

~ ~ ~

I certainly caught Parker's attention when I strolled into Rick's office dressed to impress.

"Well, well, will you look at Mr fancy pants, where's the funeral?" she sneered.

"Just dressing up to handle the bureaucratic storm, so to speak," I gloated.

"So, what did you tell Donald?" Rick asked with interest.

"It was all about Grant Lee, wasn't it? So, I informed him that the Hong Kong cops suspected him to be the brother of Lee Kok Lung, the Dragon Head of the Sun Yee On in Hong Kong. Until that can be substantiated, we agreed to keep him at arm's length for his own benefit as much as anything else," I explained.

"Well done!" Rick beamed at me.

Parker raised a single eyebrow in approval. Rick stood up from behind his desk and swivelled his computer monitor for me to see. It displayed CCTV footage of arrivals at Sydney International airport. Travellers were wheeling their bags out from behind a partition to meet their friends or relatives.

"Here comes Fatty," Rick said playfully, pointing at the screen. "Note that he's not carrying a bag."

Fatty strolled out and was greeted by two Chinese businessmen in suits.

Rick zoomed in and froze the image. "The one on the left is Jacky Chan, not the actor, but the managing director of the Fortune Garden Restaurant. The man on the right is Diamond Liu, the manager of the Fortune Garden mah-jong room. We had them in last week when we busted the casino."

"Yep, both of them were with him at the Golden Dragon yesterday. So, he arrived yesterday, then?" I inquired.

"Yes," Jess confirmed.

"He must have gone straight from the airport to the Golden Dragon... of course, the question is why, when they have their own restaurant?" Rick pondered.

"Must have had something to do with the third guy at the table who wasn't at the airport," I deduced.

"What if he's the one they've chosen to run the Golden Dragon, and that's why they met there? What if Grant Lee isn't going to take over like we thought?" Jess suggested.

"I think you've hit the nail on the head, Parker," I said, grinning at her.

"That would make complete sense. They might have also suspected that the Fortune Garden was under police surveillance after the bust," Rick added.

"Maybe it was the third guy who called me with the warning?" I contemplated.

"Why would he do that?" Jess questioned.

"When I ranted about Fatty getting out of jail to come here, he looked surprised. Maybe he's a businessman who was roped into the deal, found out who he's really dealing with from my outburst, and now wants out," I theorized.

"Could be," Rick said, stroking his chin in thought.

"Hmm, anything on the stakeout Humpty Dumpty was complaining about?" I asked them.

"He always complains about stakeouts. He doesn't like paying overtime," Rick grumbled.

"Not a soul has come out or entered the place," Jess admitted.

"Didn't you say someone was inside from the beginning?" I probed.

"It turned out to be a false alarm," she replied, shaking her head in disappointment.

"We can only keep it going for another twenty-four hours," Rick added.

"Fair enough. We can expect Ty to hear from them soon," I commented.

"Can I interest you in a coffee?" Jess offered. It was the first time she had done that — things were looking up. I figured I should dress to impress more often.

"Thanks, Parker," I said with a big Cheshire cat grin.

She waddled off to fetch the coffee.

"I think she fancies you today, Axis," Rick teased.

"Obviously, she's impressed by the threads, mate," I responded, flicking a non-existent speck of lint off my lapel.

CHAPTER TWENTY-TWO

"HOW SERIOUSLY ARE you taking this threat on your life?" Jess Parker asked as we sipped our coffees.

"Why, Parker, are you worried about me?" I joked.

There was a wicked glint in her eyes. "More like the chance of getting rid of you."

"Oh, Parker, just when I was beginning to think we were becoming friends," I said sarcastically.

Just then, "Someday Soon" started playing. "It's Ty," I said eagerly. "Yes, Ty, how's it going?"

"Okay, I'll be right over." I hung up and stood. "He's heard from them."

"Do you want us with you?" Rick asked quickly.

"No, let me talk it through with him. He clams up when you're around. I'll call you."

"Okay, good luck," Rick said.

I was halfway out the door when Parker called out to me. "I was only teasing, Stone. I don't want anything bad to happen to you."

"Thanks, Parker, that was almost convincing," I said with a sarcastic chuckle, closing the door behind me.

~ ~ ~

I could have walked to the Golden Dragon. It would have only taken fifteen minutes, but I spotted a cab and hailed it. As it turned out, we hit a couple of traffic lights, and it still took fifteen minutes and cost me twenty-six bucks plus a five-buck tip. I got a receipt for expenses. I can't believe the cost of taxis in Sydney.

~ ~ ~

Ty was pacing the floor of the private room when I entered.

"Axis, this is getting more complicated by the minute," he growled.

"Sit down, relax, mate," I said, helping him into a chair at the table. "Now, tell me why it's getting complicated."

"The two million has to be in this bank account by noon." He handed me a piece of paper with a long account number scribbled on it. "If it's not there, they will hurt Jazz."

"Did they mention the share certificate?"

"No, by the looks of it, they want the money first. I don't think that much can be arranged at such short notice."

"Have you called your accountant yet?"

"No, I was waiting for you."

"Well, this is where you have to make the choice between money and your daughter," I said slowly.

"You make it sound like a game show."

"I'm sorry if it sounds that way, but it's a fact. It's eleven ten, you've got forty-five minutes. A digital transfer only takes a couple of minutes. It's your call."

Without hesitation, he dialled his cellphone.

"Mr. Singh, the transfer of funds needs to be made at noon. I know it's not much time, but I have no control over that. I'll text you the swift and account number. Yes, please confirm when it's done. The bank knows me well enough. Yes, I will sign the mortgage whenever it's needed. Thank you, Mr. Singh. Goodbye." He glanced at me gloomily. "It is done. Now, we must continue to play the waiting game."

He ordered a bottle of bourbon.

"Looks like I've converted you to Kentucky Whiskey."

"Like you said, it's an acquired taste. Tell me, are you certain she won't be hurt?"

"I don't know, Ty. It totally depends on the sort of blokes we're dealing with."

"How did it play out in the Philippines?"

"The kidnapper was a corrupt cop with some powerful friends. He had the victim drugged out of her head, tied to a chair on a boat moored in a marina. When we made the exchange, she was wired to a bomb set to blow her and me to bits as soon as she was moved. Nick had a technical gadget that jammed the remote triggering signal to the bomb but for less than a minute. We had to locate her, cut her free of her bonds, jam the signal, and then get the hell out of there before the bomb exploded."

"Obviously, you were successful."

"The bomb went off, and the three of us were very lucky to be just far enough away to avoid serious injury."

"Was the ransom paid?"

"No, it was Nick's money. He decided at the last minute to call the bluff and rely on technology. The only trouble was, he didn't tell me he hadn't paid."

"Would that have made any difference?"

"Probably not. I've got no qualms. He did what he had to do. Unfortunately, this case is completely different."

"Why is that?"

"We had the location of the victim, and the kidnapper made the mistake of trying to do both things at once: getting the money and getting rid of the victim and me."

"So, if we had the location, would we be able to pull off a similar scenario?" he asked.

"Sure, but I think you need to consider the possible ramifications. I don't think the Sun Yee On will be very impressed if you sting them. Is ripping them off hereditary or something?"

He chuckled, "Seems it might well be. No, I'm just considering my options. I expect you might soon know the location because it's getting more serious."

"You mean by tracking Grant Lee?"

"Yes."

"I agree. I'll tell you what, if you're willing to risk Jazz and the consequences, then we need to delay the transfer of money long enough to get to them," I explained.

"What if I don't send them the full amount, say only two hundred thousand? They would get digital notification that the funds have arrived in the said account, but it would take them maybe twenty-four hours or so for them to confirm exactly how much," Ty proposed.

"And they will be expecting the full amount. Clever. You know, that might just work, but it will be a gamble."

"How do you think I ran up the debt in the first place?" he smiled.

"But you weren't using your daughter's life as collateral," I submitted.

"Damn it, Axis, we do it!" Ty snapped angrily.

"Right. But we're going to need the police on our side, do you agree?"

"Okay, but only up to a point... I only trust you," he said truthfully.

"I hear you. Okay, let's make the arrangements."

Ty got on the phone to Mr. Singh to change the directions to the bank, and I rang Rick to fill him in on everything. Rick reported that there had been movement from Grant; he was in his car right now driving towards the airport. Time was ticking. I knew from experience it would all happen in a rush, so we needed to be prepared. Rick put a team on standby. I requested that it not be SWAT, just three marksmen. He agreed.

We expected the location to be somewhere in the vicinity of Huntley Street, Alexandria, where we had picked up Fang's call before. It was a logical choice, with plenty of disused warehouses in the area, a perfect refuge to hole up with a hostage.

As noon approached, so did our anxiety. Our minds filled with doubt, justification, then more doubt. Ty was struggling with having put his only child at risk.

"I gave her a privileged upbringing, you know? Her mother died giving birth to her... best schools... never having to want for a thing, and now I put all that at risk for money," he said, his eyes reflecting self-doubt.

"I've only known your daughter for a short while, but I have grown to respect her. Don't feel shame for what you've done, Ty, because I assure you she, a chip off the old block, would do the same if the roles were reversed and you were the kidnap victim."

"You think she will understand?" he said softly.

"I know she will."

He placed a hand on my shoulder and said warmly, "Thank you for saying that, Axis."

As soon as the clock ticked over noon, Ty's phone rang. It was Mr. Singh confirming that the funds had been sent and received.

"My bet is you won't be contacted until tonight... they'll want to exchange under the cover of darkness."

"An exit strategy?" he posed.

"Yes, indeed. They need to hand over Jazz without harming her and without being caught. Rick already has an undercover team in the area we think will be the location."

"What about the share certificate?" he queried.

"You and I both know it means nothing—anyone could make up a dummy share certificate. No, Lee Kok Lung would already know that his name appears on the ASIC registry as the principal shareholder of the Golden Dragon," I explained.

"He would have accessed that online," Ty said knowingly.

"Yep. So once the cash ransom was off the table, the certificate became a red herring," I suggested.

"For what reason?"

"To buy time... what intrigues me is if Parker is right and Fatty Tung is in town for the takeover, and Grant Lee doesn't know he's here, then there's going to be one hell of a fight over this," I said, indicating the restaurant. "I expect they'll just leave Jazz somewhere and tell us the location. There won't be any handover at all."

"You're saying we will get Jazz back... the threat to you from Tung will stand, and when both parties discover they don't have the two million—"

"Yep," I smiled knowingly. "The shit will really hit the fan."

"You anticipated this, didn't you?" Ty protested.

"I had a fair idea."

"So, what is the failsafe plan?"

"First cab off the rank is to get Jazz back safely."

Once again, there was no point sitting around at the restaurant waiting for a call that I didn't expect to come until dark, so I decided to go to the nerve centre to watch things unfold.

~ ~ ~

It was a nice afternoon for a walk. When I reached the pedestrian crossing on George Street, I was waiting with the crowd for the lights to change when I remembered Mark's story about the blade in the butt and turned my head sharply when I felt someone press against me from behind. I slipped my briefcase around behind to cover my backside when I realised I was the only non-Asian in the throng on the sidewalk—it was after all Chinatown, and that fact unnerved me even more. I anticipated the lights changing and darted out in front of the horde and jogged across the wide street. I kept on going like a man on a mission, along Goulburn Street, over Elizabeth Street, across Wentworth Avenue, then Brisbane Street to Police HQ. I arrived in the lobby puffing out of breath and with a protesting ribcage. I waited at the elevator feeling stupid for being so paranoid.

Rick thought it was hilarious when I told him.

"I didn't have you pictured as the type to panic, Axis," he chuckled.

"It's not often a bloke gets a professional executioner threatening to kill him," I objected.

"No, I suppose you're right. Anyhow, you made it. What's your take on it now?" he asked.

"Are the troops in place?"

"Yes, but the kidnappers would have bailed as soon as the money hit the bank. I know because Grant got a call at exactly 12.04 from Hong Kong. It had to be confirmation from his brother."

"Last you told me, he was headed for the airport. Where did he go from there?"

"He stopped for an hour at Mascot and then drove back home to Maroubra."

"Damn! And the stakeout?" I queried.

"Well, we had a bit of luck there... A Chinaman in his mid-thirties, short but bulky, dressed in a suit, entered the apartment about fifteen minutes ago. Parker's there to supervise an arrest."

"Well, finally something goes our way."

"How's the old boy feeling about the gamble?"

"He's a punter, mate. It was basically his idea," I reminded him.

"His daughter won't be impressed when she finds out."

"No, to the contrary, I think she'd expect that from him," I posed.

"You're kidding me?" he chuckled incredulously. "Odd folk these Chinese. There's going to be hell to pay when the baddies find out they've been short-changed."

"When is Grant Lee due back at work?" I asked.

"Tomorrow."

"So, we're riding on two hopes right now. First, that we're right and Jazz will be dumped somewhere and they'll let us know where in due course, and second, Fang Peng Jian is at the apartment and will blow the whistle."

"Yeah, well, I need to make an arrest to balance the books... the shark leg case is still outstanding, so we're banking on Fang all right."

"Not good enough for Humpty Dumpty that you get the kidnap victim back unharmed?"

"For some, yes, but for him, no." He shook his head.

CHAPTER TWENTY-THREE

P ARKER ARRIVED BACK at HQ and announced she had Fang in remand.

"No hiccups?" Rick inquired.

"No, he answered the door and we cuffed him, hasn't said a word since, lips are sealed," Parker replied.

"Well, they'll certainly come unstuck when we get Jazz back to identify him," I said.

"You obviously questioned him about his part in the kidnapping and the whereabouts of the victim?" Rick queried.

"Yes, sir, like I said, he has said nothing, not a word," Parker confirmed.

Rick nodded. "Okay, we'll give him a while to stew in a cell, then we'll interview him."

"No point me hanging around then," I said, getting out of my chair.

"Oh, I don't know, I quite like you in that suit," Parker said with a cheeky grin.

"If I didn't know you better, Parker, I'd think you're trying to get into my pants," I joked.

"Not the pants, Axis, the suit," she returned serve with interest.

"You going to be all right?" Rick asked.

I patted my trusty companion strapped under my right arm. "As long as I'm with my bodyguard here, I'm okay. I'll call you when I know something. If you get anything of value out of Fang, bell me."

~ ~ ~

Out front of police HQ, "Someday Soon aroused my interest." It was Nick.

"Hey Nick, what's the latest from beautiful downtown Brisbane?"

"I'm ringing to ask you?"

"You know who I bumped into at the Golden Dragon yesterday? Fatty Tung."

"What the...? Out of jail and in Sydney?"

"And at Ty's restaurant with three other guys, two of them turn out to be Jacky Chan from the Fortune Garden and Diamond Liu..."

"The manager of the mah-jong room, yeah, I know them both. What the hell would they be doing at the Dragon?"

"I suspect the third guy was the planned successor to Ty as CEO of the restaurant."

"That would make sense, but what's that got to do with Fatty Tung?"

"Guess it's more to do with the Hong Kong chapter than the Sydney one... Anyhow, I gave him a bit of stick and he threatened me."

"When are you going to learn to keep your mouth shut, mate?"

"I know, I know, sometimes I just can't help myself... Anyhow, that said, the cops have got one of the alleged kidnappers in detention, and we're still waiting to learn the location of Jazz."

"How's Ty holding up?" he asked.

"He's fine, I'm on my way to him now from police HQ."

"Watch your back, buddy," he warned. "Tung is a ruthless killer."

"Yeah, well, I've dealt with a few of them in the past, so I'm feeling confident. What's news with you, anyway?"

"Oh, I meant to tell you... Your Suzie Wong got busted at Manila airport with a bullet in her bag."

"What! A bullet? How's that?" I snapped.

"It's the latest airport scam in Manila. A security officer slips a bullet into your bag for it to show up on the X-ray machine. Then you're taken aside by officials and asked for a bribe or charges will be laid."

"Bloody hell, you Filos think of some scams, don't you? So, what happened?"

"Dom was waiting for her at arrivals to drive her home, and after an hour, he started to get worried, so he made some inquiries. Luckily, he has a friend in customs that happened to be on duty, and he managed to fix it up for a few thousand pesos and got Suzie out. She was a bit rattled."

"Poor kid... after all she's been through. Is she all right now?"

"Yes, but she needs to hear from you, mate. You've got my home number there, give her a call when you get a chance," he suggested.

"I'll do that, mate, thanks. Call you later once we've got Jazz."

"Cool, if you need me there, just yell out, and I can be on the next plane."

"Thanks, mate."

I hung up, seriously glad to have such a good friend in Nick.

~ ~ ~

After arriving at the Golden Dragon and finding Ty absent, I learned that he was at the Fortune Garden. I immediately called him to express my concern, but Ty reassured me that he was just having a drink with an old friend and that I worried too much. He mentioned that Diamond Liu, one of the guys with Fatty Tung at the restaurant, was nearby and suggested asking him about Tung's presence in Sydney. Before I could stop him, Ty began conversing with Liu in Chinese.

When he got back on the phone, Ty informed me that Tung was indeed in Sydney for the debt settlement and the takeover of his restaurant. I was amazed that Ty had obtained such information so easily. He advised me to go home, get some rest, and wait for his call if anything happened. Reluctantly, I followed his advice and made my way home.

~ ~ ~

Sitting in my armchair with a glass of Jack Daniel's, I tried to relax and let go of the stress that had built up. Thoughts of Suzie flooded my mind, prompting me to call Nick's home. However, the conversation didn't go as expected. Suzie was crying and couldn't express herself clearly in English. It became an emotional call that left me feeling guilty. I said my goodbyes, promising to talk to her soon, but the guilt lingered.

As the orange glow of sunset filled the room, I enjoyed the warm atmosphere accompanied by a few more drinks. There was a knock at the door. It opened to a dark-haired, Chinese girl. She glided across the room toward me wearing a beautiful, hip-length, Mandarin jacket of green silk with delicate embroidery woven across the front panels. She'd forgotten to put on the bottom half of the outfit. I sat up so I could better appreciate the real-life shapeliness of her tapered legs.

She hovered just a few feet from me and then said in a husky voice, "Hello Axis, you like?"

I looked into her eyes, they were the colour of the jacket, but there was something wrong — it can't be Rosy, she'd dead!

Suddenly her eyes looked mad … stark raving mad. She opened her mouth wide like she was about to scream and exposed a mouthful of sinister unearthly pointed teeth. She hissed like a cat. Then said strangely, "I sent you… I sent you…" Another mouth projected from her own like the alien in the movie of the same name, and pointed teeth dripping with saliva gnashed and snapped at me like some sort of venomous reptile.

I sat up sharply in lather of sweat, wide-eyed with my heart pounding a like the dance floor of a disco. Relief surged when I realised it had been a terrible, vivid dream … I sighed, jumped up, strode to the bar, poured myself four fingers of JD's and skulled it. No more afternoon catnaps for me! Resonating in my mind were her words, "I sent you…" I had no idea what that meant.

~ ~ ~

About half an hour later "Someday Soon" shattered the mental image of Rosy the vampire and her cryptic message, with good news. Ty had been contacted.

"What did they say?" I asked.

"It was a different person than before."

"How do you know?"

"He had a Shanghai accent, the caller before was from Ghangzhou. He said Jazz can be collected... but only by you."

"Me, what... they asked for me by name?"

"Yes."

"That's a bit odd isn't it?"

"I thought so."

"Okay, so, where is she?"

"He said we will find her at 17A Port Access Road, White Bay."

"Rozelle. Whoa! That's a long way from Alexandria where Rick has the snipers planted."

"I think that place was... what do you call it, a red herring?"

"Yeah, seems so," I agreed.

"Oh, and he said you are to come alone, unarmed."

"Yeah, right, and pigs fly... first of all if I'm just going to collect Jazz, what would it matter if I had an army with me? Secondly, I'm not about to shoot her so, if there isn't going to be someone there to shoot me, why should I be unarmed?"

"I guess you're right, there must be a trap to set for you."

"There's only one person who wants to get square with me and that's Fatty Tung. Jazz mightn't even be there, and if she is, she might be dead."

"No! She's alive I spoke to her."

"Did she tell you anything?"

"Only that he will kill her if there are any police."

I could feel the noose tightening around my neck. Fatty was gunning for me, now that they think they have the money and the restaurant, the hostage is his to lure me.

"All right, all right... did he give you a time?"

"Yes, 9.30 p.m."

"That only gives me an hour and a half."

"What are you going to do, Axis? I didn't hire you to walk into a shootout with a gangster for only one to survive."

"It nearly always comes down to this... Just leave it to me, Ty."

"I'll send Sunny with the car to drive you."

"Who's Sunny?"

"The bodyguard who pulled the knife on you."

"Oh, that's Sunny. Good, tell him to pick me up out front of the Regal Apartments in Sussex Street at nine, and that he'll have to wait and then bring us both back, even if I'm dead. Got that?"

"Yes Axis... got it. Good luck."

I rang Rick and told him the change of plan but left out the location. They'd got nothing out of interrogating Fang. The only hope he had left of making him talk was to get Jazz to identify him. When I said I was going in alone he went off at me big time—but at the end of the day—Fatty had left us no choice. Rick pleaded for me to give him the location but as much as I'm his friend, I had to deny him—he wasn't pleased with me at all.

I finished the call with, "The next time you hear from me mate, will be to send a body bag for Fatty Tung."

CHAPTER TWENTY-FOUR

A **COLD FRONT** had moved in. I could hear the wind howling outside my apartment window. Winter had arrived in Sydney. A hip holster would be the wisest choice in the dark, easier to draw and less conspicuous. I strapped it on over my black shirt. The weather outside was getting angry; I'd need to be rugged up against it, so I pulled my black three-quarter length driza-bone coat from the wardrobe and my favourite black Fedora hat. Garbed up, I checked myself in the full-length mirror—black jeans, black R.M Williams Cuban heel boots—the waterproof coat, the hat—awesome, I was ready to rock. One last thing... I trawled through my junk-drawer for a switchblade. It was a souvenir from a job a few years back. Found it. A quick test to satisfy it was still working, and I slipped it into my coat pocket.

It was time to head downstairs to meet Sunny. I skulled a JD's for some Dutch courage, took a look around my apartment to motivate me that it wouldn't be the last time I'd see it, and bailed out.

~ ~ ~

It was indeed blowing a gale in the street outside. Sussex Street runs north to south, and at this time of year, the southerly wind can power through the canyons of the city like a dragon's breath. I stayed behind the glass lobby doors out of the elements, waiting for Sunny to arrive. There were only a few people on the street; it was too much of a fight to keep an umbrella from turning inside out, so Sussex

Street is mostly avoided. The traffic had subsided, only a few cars with glaring headlights getting the free wash from the rain. A pair of headlights flashed on the walls of the lobby and stopped out front. It had to be Sunny, so I turned up my coat collar and made a charge for the car, gripping the brim of my hat to stop it from taking off.

The rear door opened as I reached it, so I only got a spray of rain for a few seconds before I slid onto the backseat and slammed the weather out.

"Phew! What a night!" I said to Sunny behind the wheel. He just nodded. Not a big conversationalist, he drove us in silence through the tempest to Rozelle.

As we turned off Robert Street onto Port Access Road, I realised why the location had been selected: there were no streetlights—warehouses and port facilities were all dormant this time of night—it was the archetypal setting from some el cheapo Hong Kong gangster movie with the big shoot-out at the end. I thought to myself, why is my job so full of all the clichés?

A few moments later, the navigation aid told Sunny we were approaching 17A, and he slowed the car.

Sunny spoke for the first time, "That's it on the right."

I was surprised by his voice; it was half his size.

"Okay, just pull up opposite."

I couldn't see a car parked anywhere. It was a complex of six warehouses that had seen their best years and left deserted. Two old decrepit fishing trawlers were up on stilts at the water's edge, and the only light came from the ambient glow of the city in the background across the bay. The wind was being whipped up even stronger, roaring across White Bay, but at least the rain had quit.

"Are you carrying a piece?" I asked Sunny.

He leaned across to the glove compartment, opened it, and withdrew a Glock 37.

"Nice," I said. "Now listen, I'm going to check out those buildings over there for Jazz... you keep an eye on me from the car, don't get out... but if you see me in trouble or waving at you, don't hesitate to shoot whoever's giving me grief. You got that?"

His big head nodded.

"Okay, here we go," I growled to rev myself up.

I stepped out into the misty rain, and the dreadful gale hit me in the face like a wet sock. Holding the brim of my hat, I charged across the road, entered the property through an old gate swinging in the wind on rusted-out hinges, and found cover under an awning. I couldn't be bothered playing hide and seek, so I called out at the top of my voice, "Jazz, it's Axis, are you in there?" The roar of the wind was my only reply. I saw a side entrance door to the first warehouse, drew my pistol, and made for it. I hate this sort of stuff. In the movies, the music score makes a scene like this dramatic, but in real life, it's underscored by screeching corrugated iron and stuff swinging in the gale, more creepy than dramatic. With the vision of Fatty stepping out from the shadows with a gun aimed at me dominating my mind, I pulled open the door and entered the building. I wished I'd brought a torch.

Every step I made on the wooden floor echoed in the empty building. There was no one there; I could sense it. I asked myself, where would I have dumped Jazz? I'd put my money on the office building, where there would be more rooms to hide in ambush.

I slipped back outside and took in the panorama of the complex... the building in the centre was the only one with a front door, it had to be the office. Just as I headed for it, the heavens opened up. It had a porch, and I nearly slipped base over apex negotiating the four stairs up while trying to avoid the water gushing out of the rust-eroded guttering. With my back to the wall, I leaned forward to take a peek inside through a shattered window. It was the office all right—the reception at the front, and a corridor that would lead to what I estimated to be another six rooms off it.

Jazz wasn't in the front office, I could tell it was empty—but like before, if it had been me, I would have put her deeper inside to draw me in. That meant it was going to get very sticky.

I pushed the door open and with my .38 up, slipped inside and bellowed, "Jazz, are you there? It's Axis."

From a lull in the rain beating on the iron roof, I heard a muffled but frantic groan deeper inside. It had to be her.

"I hear you Jazz, keep making a noise so I can find you."

I moved into the dark corridor, listening intently for the next sound from Jazz to direct me. But the broken glass crunching under my every step, the drumming of the rain on the corrugated tin roof, the water streaming through holes in the ceiling and splashing on the floor, was making it difficult to hear anything above that cacophony.

I crossed the room, ready to shoot anything other than Jazz that moved. It was dark and difficult to find a clear path through all the fallen debris to where I figured she could be. Finally, the rain eased off enough for me to get a good read on her muffled yelps. She was in the next office to the left of the corridor, but building materials were blocking the way. I kept on walking in a kind of blind man's shuffle—it was slow going. My head bumped something solid, which hurt, and my exploring fingers came up with the answer—it was a part of the collapsed ceiling. Then, Fatty made a mistake, he shuffled, and in a moment of quiet, I detected the slightest sound of glass crunch under his shoes. He was in the office directly opposite Jazz, waiting, watching... probably with a clear shot at me if I tried to enter through the only door that led to her. I had one advantage: it was just as tough for him to see me as it was for me to see him. I had to beat him at his own game. I removed my hat and coat... got down on hands and knees and crawled along the corridor on my belly like a snake. The rain started up again, drumming on the roof, and that covered me enough to move quicker. I made it past the entrance to the room he was in. As I got to my feet, a lightning flash illuminated the corridor, and in those milliseconds, for the first time, I could see what I was up against. Right outside the door to Fatty's room on my side of the corridor was a wooden office desk smashed in half. If I could get behind it and get a bead on Fatty during a flash of lightning,

I might just be able to peel off a shot at him. No way he'd expect me to shoot from there.

Thunder rumbled. I worked out the lightning flashes were three minutes apart, the next one would be my signal to scoot to the broken desk using the thunderclap that followed as cover for any sound I'd make. From there, I could line him up for a shot during the next flash. It was a roll of the dice, but it was the best option.

The flash came, the rain drummed, and I scurried to the desk... I was lucky the ensuing thunderclap covered the clunk of me knocking the desk with my knee as I reached it. Ouch! It hurt. Shielded behind the desk, I aimed blindly into the dark at where I figured he was and counted down with my heart in my throat for the next flash of lightning.

It came right on time—I sighted him and fired—it was over in the blink of an eye, but I had no idea whether I'd hit him. I listened for a sound you'd expect to hear from someone wounded but heard nothing. There was no alternative but to wait for the next flash. The thunder resounded, and the entire place shuddered. Jazz squawked. I figured after hearing the gunshot she must be wondering which of us was hit.

I took aim at the same spot, ready for the next flash.

The flash came, but there was no-one there. He'd moved—I figured there must be a back door to that room. It was my chance to make a break to get to Jazz. I waited for the lightning to guide me, and when it flashed, I rushed in through the door and found her hog-tied and gagged in the corner of the room. It was lucky she was in her underwear, and it was white, otherwise it would have been difficult to find her in the dark.

Thunder sounded, it was more distant—the storm was passing. I drew my flick-knife and cut her free of her bonds. After I helped her up, I removed the gag, and she hugged me.

Weeping, she pleaded emotionally, "Oh Axis... thank God!"

"Come on, this guy is still on the loose."

I led her into the corridor, found my coat, and put it around her. I picked up my hat, and then we rushed into the front office.

"See the car," I pointed. "Sunny is there. You'll have to make a run for it... but lose the coat, otherwise our friend might take a pot shot at you, thinking it's me."

"Okay, I can do it. What are you going to do?"

"I'm going to hunt the bastard down and blow a hole in him."

"Why don't we just go?" she pleaded.

"Because he'll only come after me... there can only be one winner here tonight."

"Who is he?"

"Long story, but he's a Triad hit-man from Hong Kong. It seems I offended him enough there to warrant being whacked."

I walked her out onto the porch. I could see bloody footprints and realised the broken glass had lacerated her bare feet.

"Your feet are cut, can you run?"

"Can't feel a thing... are you on about feet again?"

"Can't help myself," I chuckled. "Okay, when I say go, drop the coat and run like the devil."

I waited until I felt the moment was right and then said, "Okay, go!"

She slipped out of the coat and took off running like a gazelle into the light rain.

The rear car door opened as she reached it, and she disappeared safely inside. I put on my coat and hat for the hunt. I slipped back outside and took in the panorama of the complex... the building in the centre was the only one with a front door, it had to be the office. Just as I headed for it, the heavens opened up. It had a porch, and I nearly slipped base over apex negotiating the four stairs up while trying to avoid the water gushing out of the rust-eroded guttering. With my back to the wall, I leaned forward to take a peek inside through a shattered window. It was the office all right—the reception at the front, and a corridor that would lead to what I estimated to be another six rooms off it.

Jazz wasn't in the front office, I could tell it was empty—but like before, if it had been me, I would have put her deeper inside to draw me in. That meant it was going to get very sticky.

I pushed the door open and with my .38 up, slipped inside and bellowed, "Jazz, are you there? It's Axis."

From a lull in the rain beating on the iron roof, I heard a muffled but frantic groan deeper inside. It had to be her.

"I hear you Jazz, keep making a noise so I can find you."

I moved into the dark corridor, listening intently for the next sound from Jazz to direct me. But the broken glass crunching under my every step, the drumming of the rain on the corrugated tin roof, the water streaming through holes in the ceiling and splashing on the floor, was making it difficult to hear anything above that cacophony.

I crossed the room, ready to shoot anything other than Jazz that moved. It was dark and difficult to find a clear path through all the fallen debris to where I figured she could be. Finally, the rain eased off enough for me to get a good read on her muffled yelps. She was in the next office to the left of the corridor, but building materials were blocking the way. I kept on walking in a kind of blind man's shuffle—it was slow going. My head bumped something solid, which hurt, and my exploring fingers came up with the answer—it was a part of the collapsed ceiling. Then, Fatty made a mistake, he shuffled, and in a moment of quiet, I detected the slightest sound of glass crunch under his shoes. He was in the office directly opposite Jazz, waiting, watching... probably with a clear shot at me if I tried to enter through the only door that led to her. I had one advantage: it was just as tough for him to see me as it was for me to see him. I had to beat him at his own game. I removed my hat and coat... got down on hands and knees and crawled along the corridor on my belly like a snake. The rain started up again, drumming on the roof, and that covered me enough to move quicker. I made it past the entrance to the room he was in. As I got to my feet, a lightning flash illuminated the corridor, and in those milliseconds, for the first time, I could see what I was up against. Right outside the door to Fatty's room on my side of the corridor was a wooden office desk smashed in half. If I could get behind it and get a bead on Fatty during a flash of lightning, I might just be able to peel off a shot at him. No way he'd expect me to shoot from there.

Thunder rumbled. I worked out the lightning flashes were three minutes apart, the next one would be my signal to scoot to the broken desk using the thunderclap that followed as cover for any sound I'd make. From there, I could line him up for a shot during the next flash. It was a roll of the dice, but it was the best option.

The flash came, the rain drummed, and I scurried to the desk... I was lucky the ensuing thunderclap covered the clunk of me knocking the desk with my knee as I reached it. Ouch! It hurt. Shielded behind the desk, I aimed blindly into the dark at where I figured he was and counted down with my heart in my throat for the next flash of lightning.

It came right on time—I sighted him and fired—it was over in the blink of an eye, but I had no idea whether I'd hit him. I listened for a sound you'd expect to hear from someone wounded but heard nothing. There was no alternative but to wait for the next flash. The thunder resounded, and the entire place shuddered. Jazz squawked. I figured after hearing the gunshot she must be wondering which of us was hit.

I took aim at the same spot, ready for the next flash.

The flash came, but there was no-one there. He'd moved—I figured there must be a back door to that room. It was my chance to make a break to get to Jazz. I waited for the lightning to guide me, and when it flashed, I rushed in through the door and found her hog-tied and gagged in the corner of the room. It was lucky she was in her underwear, and it was white, otherwise it would have been difficult to find her in the dark.

Thunder sounded, it was more distant—the storm was passing. I drew my flick-knife and cut her free of her bonds. After I helped her up, I removed the gag, and she hugged me.

Weeping, she pleaded emotionally, "Oh Axis... thank God!"

"Come on, this guy is still on the loose."

I led her into the corridor, found my coat, and put it around her. I picked up my hat, and then we rushed into the front office.

"See the car," I pointed. "Sunny is there. You'll have to make a run for it... but lose the coat, otherwise our friend might take a pot shot at you, thinking it's me."

"Okay, I can do it. What are you going to do?"

"I'm going to hunt the bastard down and blow a hole in him."

"Why don't we just go?" she pleaded.

"Because he'll only come after me... there can only be one winner here tonight."

"Who is he?"

"Long story, but he's a Triad hit-man from Hong Kong. It seems I offended him enough there to warrant being whacked."

I walked her out onto the porch. I could see bloody footprints and realised the broken glass had lacerated her bare feet.

"Your feet are cut, can you run?"

"Can't feel a thing... are you on about feet again?"

"Can't help myself," I chuckled. "Okay, when I say go, drop the coat and run like the devil."

I waited until I felt the moment was right and then said, "Okay, go!"

She slipped out of the coat and took off running like a gazelle into the light rain.

The rear car door opened as she reached it, and she disappeared safely inside. I put on my coat and hat for the hunt.

CHAPTER TWENTY-FIVE

A **SHOT RANG** out, and a bullet ricocheted off the building, missing my face by only six inches. It did something other than scare the living crap out of me: it gave away his position. With stealth, I hugged the façade of the building with my back and crept along it to stop him from getting a clean shot at me. When I came to the last building, I knew he must be near where he'd peeled off that last shot. I figured he was just around the corner of the building.

I heard the car window open and glanced in time to see Sunny's arm appear and aim the Glock in my direction. Immediately, I knew what he was thinking. The Glock 37, a .45 calibre handgun, not only packs a high-velocity wallop, but it's bloody loud. It has a ten-round magazine. I counted off his shots, as he fired the seventh into the corner of the building, just three feet from me. It was not only good grouping, but it confirmed Fatty was there. Sunny could see him... plus, the salvo provided me cover to make a move. I waved my arm furiously at Sunny and then took off at speed. Once clear of the corner of the building, I dived onto the ground, paratrooper rolled on my left shoulder, and came up on one knee with my .38 aimed at Fatty. He was on his knees no more than twenty feet from me, hugging the wall of the building.

I shouted at him, "Drop it!"

I could see he was hit by the way he was favouring his left arm— my shot earlier must have winged him. The seconds ticked by—he was wavering, holding his pistol up, but not aimed at me. He knew if he tried to make a move, I'd fire... and I wouldn't miss at that range. He slowly lowered his gun hand in surrender and then struggled to his feet. I stood up with my gun trained on him. No way I was going to trust the bloke.

"Drop your gun, Fatty!" I demanded.

"Fuck you!" he shouted and whipped his gun up to fire. I squeezed off a shot before he could, and blood, bone, hair, and brain matter painted a gruesome picture on the faded yellow brick wall behind him. With a .38 hole in his cheek just under his left eye and the back of his head missing, his legs crumbled, and he hit the turf, dead meat.

I holstered my weapon, dusted myself off, turned my back on the corpse, and while walking back to the car, I drew my phone and speed dialled Rick. "Hey, yep, it's me... I live again. Better send the meat wagon to 17A Port Access Road, Rozelle, got that? Yeah, they can tag the body bag Fatty Tung... Yeah, I'll wait for them... Yep, she's fine... Okay, I'll bring her there in the morning. Thanks, mate, ciao."

When I climbed into the car, I was surprised to find Jazz dressed. Sunny had thought to bring her a change of clothes.

"Much obliged, Sunny, your cover shots did the trick."

He turned from the driver's seat and beamed me a big gold-toothed smile. "No worries, boss, it was Miss Sun's idea."

I called Ty and put Jazz on the phone to speak to her dad in Chinese.

Ten minutes later, I noticed the flashing lights of approaching cop cars: a meat wagon and a patrol car. When they stopped, I got out, introduced myself, and then walked them over to the corpse. One of them was forensics, and she started clicking photographs of the blood spatter, corpse, and the general crime scene. I was then required to recite an account of events into a hand recorder to be time-stamped as evidence and then hand over my pistol for ballistics.

The cop then took a statement from Jazz and Sunny, and Sunny's gun. After that, we were finally free to go.

Jazz cuddled up beside me with her head on my shoulder, and we sat in silence on the rear seat of the car all the way back to town. Ty had insisted on bringing Jazz to the restaurant, so Sunny stopped at the rear entrance. We got out, and Jazz led me through the kitchen to the private room. You would have expected a teary reception, but no, it was as though Jazz had only been away for a weekend holiday. Odd folks, these Chinese, I thought. By then, it was after midnight. I downed a couple of JDs and was feeling pretty knackered, totally not in the mood for hearing Ty and Jazz babbling on in Cantonese. For me, her full account of the kidnapping could wait until tomorrow.

"Sorry to interrupt, but I'm pretty tired, so I'm going to bail and hit the hay," I said, cutting into their conversation. "Jazz, you'll be required at police HQ at 9 a.m."

"That'll be fine. Want us to pick you up out front of your apartments at 8:30?" she asked.

"Good-oh, see you then, goodnight, Ty."

"Thank you, Axis," Ty said. "Well done. I knew we could count on you."

"It'll be in the bill," I joked.

As I walked through the empty restaurant, I noticed Sunny sitting alone at a table eating.

I rested my hand on his big shoulder and said, "You did well tonight, Sunny."

"No worries, boss," he smiled, and then went back to his congee. Then he looked up with an afterthought. "You want me to drive you home?"

"No thanks, mate. The walk will do me good."

~ ~ ~

It wasn't raining or windy outside. I looked up at the sky, and the clouds parted for a big full moon to beam down on me. I thought, it's no wonder there are so many lunatics out tonight.

There was a winter nip in the air that caused me to make the ten-minute walk to my apartment block in record time.

When I got inside, I rang Nick.

"Hey Nick, yep, I made it, but Fatty didn't."

"Jesus, Axis, are you okay? Tell me about it?"

"Fatty had taken control of the kidnapping and had Jazz at an old disused warehouse at White Bay docks. She was in a half-demolished office in her underwear, hogtied and gagged, and Fatty was waiting for me."

"A trap?"

"You bet it. Anyhow, I managed to get a shot and winged him. He took off... I got Jazz to the safety of the car and then went after him. Ty's bodyguard Sunny was my driver, and he hung out of the limo window with a Glock 37, giving me the cover to corner Fatty. I gave the guy a chance to surrender, but he tried to take a pot-shot at me, and I hit him first."

"Dead?"

"As a doornail, he's got his own slab in the city morgue right now."

"Wow, sounds like a close call. What's the next move?"

"Debriefing at police HQ with Rick and Parker in the morning. That's when we'll get the whole box and dice from Jazz. They're holding Fang, so I expect they'll get her to ID him, and that might open him up, but I somehow doubt it."

"Yeah, I'm with you... he won't risk it. If he grassed on them, his gang would hunt him down and kill him."

"What's the news at your end?"

"We're flying to Uluru tomorrow afternoon. Why don't you meet us there? Lola's coming as well."

"No, man, this case isn't done yet. We still have to sort out Grant Lee and who killed Rosy... Besides, what's going to happen when the

Dragon Head discovers Fatty's dead and he only got two hundred grand instead of two mill?"

"I spoke to Ty earlier tonight. He rang me just to talk and said he only sent fifty thousand."

"He's a sly bugger. That's the problem with him. Just when you think you can trust the guy, he does something like that and then keeps it from me... reminds me of someone else—"

"I thought you'd say that. I guess it's in our Chinese DNA to take a discount... anyhow, you're damn right. Lee Kok Lung isn't going to be impressed when he finds out. Might be a good idea to call Zhong tomorrow to tell him what happened to Fatty. He'll be pleased... plus, he could alert immigration to keep an eye out in case Lee sends another hitman."

"I don't think he'll do that. It's more likely he'll get someone from here to take out Ty. He won't find out I killed Fatty. He'll think it was the cops, and I'll see to it that's how it appears. That way, I'll be clear of reprisals."

"Sound thinking. All right, mate, glad you're okay. You've done a top job again, Kemosabe."

"Thanks, Nick. Oh, by the way, I rang Suzie, but I couldn't stop her blubbering long enough to get a word in."

"Yes, I've had reports she has been upset. You need to see her, Axis."

"Mate, the last thing I need now are problems of a feminine kind," I admitted.

"I thought you told me that was an occupational hazard," he said smugly.

"Goodbye, Nick. Have a good time at Uluru, and say hi to the girls for me."

I hung up, poured myself a JD, kicked off my boots, and sat on the couch with my feet up on the coffee table. It was only ten thirty in Hong Kong, so I decided to give Zhong a call.

"Hey, Zhong, it's Axis."

"Hello, Axis. How is it all going?"

"I just thought you should know that Fatty Tung is in the Sydney morgue with a bullet in his head."

"You've made my day, Axis," he said cheerfully. "Did the kidnapping turn out okay?"

"Yes, we got Jazz Sun back in one piece, and now all we have to worry about is Lee Kok Lung's brother and any reprisals."

"What do you mean by reprisals?"

"Well, when Lee Kok Lung realises that he's been shortchanged and that his Red Pole is dead, he might well react."

"No, you can rest assured nothing will come of it. He has lost two men on this deal. It wasn't worth it... he'll now leave it up to his brother to sort out."

"I'm happy to take you on advisement, mate. You have all the experience with these dudes. I'm all at sea trying to understand them."

He chuckled, then said reassuringly, "Let me know if you need anything else, Axis."

"Okay, Zhong. Take it easy, mate."

I put my phone on the coffee table, drained my glass of the last drip of JD, and then dragged myself off to the sack for a well-earned snore.

~ ~ ~

The skies were clear, and the morning sun streamed into The Grind Café. I had just finished my morning coffee when a limo pulled up outside. I paid and headed out in time to find Sunny fending off a parking cop. We drove off before he could get a ticket.

Poised on the back seat, Jazz looked stunning, dressed in a red cheongsam split all the way up, revealing a sexy naked leg, and her hair held up in a bun by two black and gold lacquered chopsticks. Her bright red lipstick and matching fingernails almost completed the look until I noticed her red toenails protruding from her red Christian Louboutin T-Strap sandals.

"You look stunning today," I complimented her.

She looked at me over the top of her sunglasses and replied, "Thank you, Axis. No suit for you?"

"No, my uniform is black jeans, a tee, black leather jacket, and sneakers."

"Hmm, macho," she said huskily, raising her thin eyebrows.

Sunny dropped us off out front of Police HQ, and I led Jazz inside to the elevator.

On the way up, she asked, "We haven't talked over what happened at all. Do I tell the truth or leave some out?"

"No need to leave anything out, just be upfront," I reassured her.

"What about the money transfer? Have you told them how much Daddy actually sent?"

"Not yet. I only found out last night when I rang Nick. Your father hasn't been very forthcoming with important details like that."

CHAPTER TWENTY-SIX

WE STEPPED OUT of the elevator at Homicide and walked through the open plan office towards Rick's private room at the back. Heads turned to gawk at Jazz, who strutted her stuff like a high-fashion catwalk model. Rick greeted us with a wink and a sly grin, while Parker seemed cold, possibly due to some feminine rivalry.

After introductions, we all sat down, and Rick turned on a recorder, ID'ing it and date-stamping it for evidence. He signalled Jazz to begin her account of the kidnapping.

Jazz appeared intimidated by the recording but proceeded confidently, wringing her hands. She started, "I was in the bedroom when I heard a noise in the lounge room. Thinking it was probably just the guard getting a drink of water or something, I went out to check. Three guys with stockings covering their faces were tying the cop up. His face was all battered and bloody. I think he was unconscious. One of them had a knife. He spoke to me in Cantonese, with a thick southern accent. The other two stayed silent. I figured they were all armed, so I wasn't about to make a scene. The guy with the knife took hold of my arm, and with the other two following behind, they took us down in the elevator and out to a car that was illegally parked out front of the Connaught. Another guy, the driver, was behind the wheel with the engine running."

Rick asked, "Was he masked as well?"

"No, but I didn't have time to see his face because as soon as they got me onto the back seat, they pulled a hood over my head."

Parker inquired, "Okay, is there anything you can think of to identify any of them?"

Jazz replied, "No, they all stayed silent while we drove somewhere... it felt like an hour with the hood on, but it was probably only twenty-five minutes. When we got to wherever it was, the car went over a bumpy section, then stopped. Someone got out, and I heard a garage roller door open, and then the car went inside. The garage door closed, they all got out except the guy next to me... he tied my hands, legs, and then gagged me. He left the hood on me, pushed me down onto the seat, and left me there. I heard a door open and close. That's where I stayed until last night."

Parker asked, "Did they give you food and water?"

"Yes, at meal times, the same guy returned with a bowl of rice and water. He would help me out of the car to have a pee."

"So, he untied you?"

"No, he took the hood off, pulled down my panties, and sat me on a drum that had a plank across it. When I finished, he pulled up my panties and put me back in the car. He left the hood off... I could breathe better then."

"Was he always wearing a stocking over his head?" Parker questioned.

"Yes."

"And wearing the same clothes?" Parker added.

"No, different each day, but only slightly."

"So, we can assume this guy probably wasn't staying there," Rick posed.

"No, I think he might have been living there," I supposed.

"I agree, I think he was living there because sometimes I could smell scented soap on him, like he'd only just taken a shower," Jazz explained.

"Would you recognise this guy if you saw him again... with a stocking over his head, of course?" Parker asked.

"Maybe, but I can't say for certain," Jazz admitted.

"You didn't overhear any conversation at all, you know... talking on phones, chatting a distance away... anything?" Rick probed.

She thought about it, then shook her head. "No, nothing."

Our hopes sank as it appeared the kidnappers knew what they were doing and covered their tracks professionally.

"There is one thing," Jazz said, "but it's only small."

"Go on, Jazz. It doesn't matter how small," I encouraged her.

"In the morning, they gave me congee. It's a traditional Chinese breakfast that's like porridge, only made from rice. Well, it wasn't ordinary congee... it was jook, which is Cantonese congee and it takes a long time to cook."

"What are you saying, Jazz?" Parker asked.

"Well, I doubt they could have cooked it at the premises. Jook is difficult to make. It must have come from a nearby Chinese restaurant."

The realisation hit me, and I exclaimed, "Fortune Garden! They must have been near it."

"Well, if they were at Alexandria, where we triangulated Fang's call, they would only be ten, fifteen minutes away, max," Rick declared.

"Does that help?" Jazz asked.

"Just more ammunition to use on Fang Peng Jian, whom we have in custody," Rick said.

"How much longer can you hold him, Rick?" I questioned.

"Only till the end of the day."

"So, he's said nothing, not a word?" I challenged.

"Mate, he just sat there with a face like a slapped bum," Rick scoffed.

"Sir, I'd like to ask Miss Sun a couple more questions," Parker chimed in. Rick nodded, and she continued. "Jazz, tell us about when they moved you last night."

"Okay, I could tell there were only two of them, and one was a new guy. He wasn't local; his clothes smelled of mothballs. They left me on the back seat of the car, tied up, and put the hood back over my head. They sat on the front seats. Someone opened the roller door, and we drove out. We drove for about forty minutes in pouring rain. We went over a bridge; I could tell by the sound... then shortly after that, we stopped, and the mothball guy dragged me out of the car. He had calloused hands and was rough with me, not like the other guy before who had smooth hands... there was lightning and thunder. He turned my back to him, took my hood off, untied my hands and feet, and then stripped me of my clothes and shoes, leaving me in my underwear. Then he put the hood back on me and retied my hands. The car drove off with my clothes, and he led me inside a building. There was broken glass on the floor; I could feel it cutting the soles of my feet. When I complained, he just dragged me harder. I was wet and freezing. He stopped in a room, pushed me down to the floor, and then took off the hood, so I could see."

"Did you see his face?" Parker asked.

"No, it was too dark. But I could see he had a gun in his hand. After that, Axis turned up."

"The hood was uncovered from the crime scene, sir, and Fatty Tung's clothes did smell of mothballs," Parker concluded.

"Okay, thanks, Jazz. All we need now from you is to identify the man we have in custody. Parker, could you go down and prepare the suspects, please?" Rick checked his wristwatch. "We'll be good to go in fifteen minutes."

"Yes, sir," Parker said as she got up and left.

"What are you thinking, Axis?" Rick asked, aware that I was mulling it all over.

"Ah... I'm just wondering how we can use the Fortune Garden congee connection," I said.

"Jook, it's called jook," Jazz corrected me.

"That's it. Let's tell Fang we're holding a cook from the Fortune Garden kitchen whom we caught on CCTV delivering food to a warehouse in Alexandria."

"No mate, it wouldn't work... look, the truth of it is if Jazz can't ID him, we're sunk. We'll have to let him go," I said, accepting the reality.

"Fair enough, I figured it was probably a long shot anyway," Rick replied.

We sat in silence, contemplating Jazz's story and searching for clues. Eventually, Rick checked his watch and decided it was time to head down to the interview rooms.

"I'm a little nervous," Jazz admitted in the elevator. "Everything seems to be riding on me recognising this guy."

"Calm down kiddo, either you'll know him or you won't. Just be honest," I said, hoping to comfort her.

"We will also be studying him to see if he recognises you. Parker is trained to do that," Rick added.

That seemed to settle her nerves a little more.

We left the elevator and entered a room where Rick instructed us to take a seat. A few minutes later, a uniformed cop led six men into the room in single file, setting up an identity parade. Each man stood under a number stencilled on the back wall. Parker entered through the same door and sat at the front, close to the line-up. The suspects were ordered to face forward, and they all appeared to be of similar height and stature, all Chinese.

"Take your time to study each face, Jazz," Rick told her.

Jazz nodded and began studying the faces. After five minutes, Parker stood up and handed out a stocking to each man, instructing them to pull it over their heads. I had no idea which one of them was Fang.

Jazz took her time deliberating, but it was clear she was struggling. Eventually, Parker nodded to the uniformed officer, who then escorted the suspects out of the room. Parker joined us, and Rick asked Jazz, "Well, what do you think?"

"I could have seen any one of them before at the Golden Dragon, but no, when they put the stocking on, the guy I caught only a short glimpse of certainly wasn't among them," Jazz replied.

"Are you quite certain, Jazz?" Parker pressed.

"Positive," Jazz said emphatically.

Rick glanced at me, and I could see the disappointment on his face. "Fang was number five."

Feeling defeated, I sat with my elbows on my knees and my face in my hands. Rick was pacing the floor, Jazz was feeling like she'd spoilt the party.

Not wanting to give up entirely, Parker asked enthusiastically, "So, where do we go from here?"

I looked up from my hands and muttered, "For a mug of strong, freshly brewed coffee, I reckon."

A short while later, we found ourselves sitting around a table in a quaint little café near Police HQ. Four mugs of coffee arrived, and we all hoped that the caffeine would spark some inspiration for our next move.

"I don't know about you, but I'm fresh out of ideas," Rick admitted.

"Do you have a suspect for Uncle Chiang's murder?" Jazz asked.

"No, nor the murder of Rosy Tong... we have our suspicions, but we don't have enough evidence for an arrest," Rick conceded.

The melancholy settled in when suddenly Ty's voice came through the phone, playing "Someday Soon". He reported that someone had threatened his life, providing us with the break we needed—a contact with the bad guys. The game was still in play, but now with a new and heightened threat. Ty was shaken, taking refuge in his Darling Harbour apartment with two armed bodyguards for protection.

"What exactly was said, Ty?" I asked, putting him on speaker so that everyone could hear.

"He said it wasn't enough money, that I had robbed him, and if I don't pay up, he will feed me to the sharks like he did my brother," Ty relayed.

"Anything else?" I inquired.

"He said everyone I know is in danger, and he can wait, for a year, even more if he wants to... he is in no hurry. The sooner I pay up, the safer everyone will be. It's a siege, Axis," Ty explained.

"Did you recognise his voice?" Rick asked.

"No, I didn't recognise it," Ty replied.

"Okay, we'll be there within the hour," I assured him.

"No hurry, I'm not going anywhere," Ty said with a sense of desolation.

I pocketed my phone and looked at Rick. "Well, the beat goes on."

"Sure does, but it doesn't get any easier," Rick observed.

"And now he's threatening Dad and me?" Jazz murmured.

"Yes, and anyone else associated with you," I confirmed.

Jazz's remark and expression had put me off my coffee.

CHAPTER TWENTY-SEVEN

"**HE'S SAYING HE** means business, especially by stating he's prepared to wait Ty out," Parker stated. She wasn't wrong.

"Like Ty said... a siege. Look, if we agree that Grant Lee is behind this, then we need to come up with a way of flushing him out into the open. He's all we've got," I proposed, assertively.

"Too true," Parker responded. "When the hunter becomes the hunted."

"Waxing lyrical, Parker?" I teased.

"Not really. What I'm saying is we've been waiting for him to make a move and because of that, we've been treating him as the hunter. Now we need to hunt him... turn the tables on him," she explained, making a spinning motion with her hands to demonstrate.

"What do you have in mind?" Rick questioned.

She smiled cunningly, "Well, like my dear old dad used to say, it's the devil you know. So let's invite him into our ranks on the case and then wait for him to make a mistake."

It was an epiphany, a moment of divine inspiration, and we revelled in it. Rick and Parker raced back to HQ to set the plan in motion, while Jazz and I went searching for Sunny to get a ride to Ty's apartment.

~ ~ ~

If Jazz's Connaught apartment was the Ritz, then Ty's sixty-first floor penthouse apartment in the World Tower was, by comparison,

Buckingham Palace. Upon entering, I was immediately struck by the 180-degree spectacular view of Sydney. It was breathtaking. Darling Harbour on one side, Sydney Harbour, the Opera House, and the Harbour Bridge on the other. Lounging back on a massive black leather couch, dressed in a robe and looking like King Farouk, was Ty.

"Come in, come in. Sit down, Axis. Jazz, get him a drink, that's a good lass," he ordered.

Jazz didn't seem impressed by the command but obliged anyway. Sunny joined the other two bodyguards on the balcony.

"Nice chunk of real estate, Ty," I commented, looking around.

"It's convenient," he responded, somewhat cockily. "So, our problem didn't vanish with the death of the Red Pole, did it?"

"Did you expect it to after only paying fifty grand?" I countered, filled with scorn.

I watched Jazz go to the bar. It was equipped to handle a three-day convention of alcoholics. She carried two glasses back, handed one to me, and then sat in an armchair facing me. I could smell the JD.

"Cheers to beating the bad guys," I raised my glass.

"I don't suppose the police have any ideas, do they?" Ty asked stiffly.

"More than you'd expect, Ty. After all, they still have two murders to solve."

"What are they going to do about this new threat? I don't want to be imprisoned in my own home," he grumbled bitterly.

"If you'd paid the correct amount, you probably wouldn't be having this problem, Ty," I shot back.

He stood up, fuming.

"I don't pay you to chastise me, Stone!" he shouted savagely.

"You pay me for my advice, and you put everyone at risk by short-paying the ransom and keeping it quiet. I put my life on the line for you, old fella, and I expect to be told the truth. Now sit down, your display of anger, like a peacock on heat, means nothing to me.

If you want help then dump the attitude, otherwise pay me out and I walk," I retorted harshly.

He gave me a dark glare and then sat back down on the couch, brooding.

"He's right, father. He's all you've got, so I'd treat him a lot better if I were you. He saved my life, did he not?"

Ty seemed to take her statement onboard and calmed down.

"Please accept my apology, Axis. I'm out of line. I should have told you about the payment. Please stay on the case, we need you."

"Okay, apology accepted. Look, Ty, I don't know any better alternative than for you to stay holed up here for the next few days. We need to give the cops a chance to flush the villain out. You're safe here. Can Jazz stay here as well?"

"I'd rather not," she responded crisply.

"I'll put some bodyguards on her, Sunny can take care of that," Ty offered.

"You'll have to stay in your apartment then, Jazz," I added.

"I can handle that," she agreed.

"Who else is there in your family?" I inquired.

"Only Sherri, my uncle's daughter. She's the same age as me and lives in Rockdale."

"Is she married? Does she work?" I queried.

Ty and Jazz shared a sheepish glance.

"No, she's single. She owns and operates a massage parlour in Rockdale. We have nothing to do with her," Ty stated dismissively.

Obviously, she was the black sheep of the family, just as Chiang had been.

"Would she know her father is dead?"

"We don't know," Ty answered dismissively.

"Okay, give me her contact details. I'll go and see her today."

"Why?" Jazz asked.

"Because I think she'd be next on the list to be hit," I stated assertively. "He'll take out the easiest mark to get at as an example of his reach, and she's the best candidate."

"You've got to be kidding, just phone her and tell her. There's no need for you to go to any trouble," Ty argued.

"You don't seem to be taking the threat very seriously when it comes to other people, Ty," I criticised.

"She's a good for nothing, Axis, not worth the trouble," he snapped.

It was similar to the dismissive way he'd referred to poor Rosy when I first mentioned her.

"Let me be the judge of that," I responded firmly, put off by his disparagement of his niece.

"She doesn't pay your fee, Axis, I do, and I say she's not worth the trouble," Ty declared emphatically.

I looked him straight in the eyes, "Think about this, Ty. She might just represent our best chance of catching this bastard."

Even with his lack of empathy, he could see the logic in that suggestion.

"You aim to use her as bait," Jazz said smugly.

I raised an eyebrow at them, "I guess you could put it like that."

~ ~ ~

I took a cab to 93A Railway Street, Rockdale, a dinky little shop with a sign out front that read Magic Hands Massage. The front window and door were covered in Chinese symbols. I opened the door, and a bell rang. I was immediately overcome by a powerful waft of Jasmine.

A stunning Chinese woman appeared from behind a partition, smiled warmly, and then said in broken English, "Hello, sir, you come for massage? I give happy ending with a half-hour massage, just seventy dollar."

"Are you Sherri Sun?"

"Yes," she half-smiled, but with a wrinkled brow.

"I'm Axis Stone, a private detective. Can we talk somewhere more intimate?"

"Yes, come into my parlour," she said in a cliché, dropping the phony broken English.

She led me into a cubicle, and I sat on the edge of the massage table while she sat in a chair and crossed her long bare legs. I glanced at her sandaled feet. It seemed that beautiful petite feet ran in the Sun family. If ever I needed a massage, you can be sure I'd be calling on Sherri Sun.

"What do you want to ask me?" She shot me a wry smile. "I hope I haven't offended some gentleman's wife."

"No, nothing like that... I'm working for your uncle, Ty Sun."

Her expression soured, like she'd just tasted something gross.

"Is this about my dad?"

"Yes, in part."

"I already know he is dead. The police contacted me."

"I'm sorry, Miss Sun."

"Don't be. We're an estranged family, dysfunctional, I suppose you'd call it. Ty and his daughter don't approve of me or my vocation."

"Miss Sun... I'm not here to judge you."

"Please, call me Sherri."

"The people who murdered your father have threatened the lives of the Sun family, which includes you. That's what I'm here to tell you."

"For the crimes of my family, the same who frown on me for what I do, my life is being threatened? That's a little ironic, don't you think, Mr Stone?" she said forcefully, punctuated by a curt smile.

"Yes, I'd have to agree with you."

"So, what do you want me to do?"

"I want you to help me catch the gangsters that murdered your father and his girlfriend."

"Oh, they killed Rosy as well? She was a good kid, worked here for twelve months until her family found out and told Ty. He took her away to be his and then turned her into my father's concubine. I think she was better off working here, no strings attached, than being Ty's town bike... at least she'd still be alive. I am sorry that she's dead."

Her remorse was genuine.

"You make sense, Sherri. What do you say... will you help?"

"I'll do it for Rosy."

"Thank you, I knew her as well, she was a lovely girl."

"If you need me to lure a man?" She grinned amorously. "I'm good at that."

"I bet you are," I mumbled under my breath. "Can you come with me now to meet the police on the case?"

"This is my business. I can open and close when I like. Just give me a minute to change." She stopped at the curtain. "Sure you don't want a massage first?"

"Not tonight, honey," I said sadly.

After a sexy wink, she disappeared behind the curtain. I liked her; she was sassy.

She called out from somewhere out back, "I suppose Ty and Jazz have locked themselves in their apartments with armed guards."

"You've got it."

"The police told me I should inherit my father's apartment, but apparently Ty thinks it belongs to him."

"Isn't there a will?"

"Yes, unfortunately for Ty, it's in my father's will. I just don't know if I want to live there."

The curtain opened, and an even more stunning woman glided back into the small room. She was dressed in a silver cheongsam split up to the hip, exposing a pair of magnificent bare legs. Around her shoulders, she wore a long, light grey cashmere shawl. Her hair was up, which showed off her lovely, long, tapered neck.

She beamed me a smile that bespoke her self-awareness. "I'm ready. Shall we go then?"

I took hold of her arm and walked her outside to catch a taxi to Police HQ.

~ ~ ~

On the way in the cab, I thought, what are all the cops at homicide going to think this time when I walk in with Sherri hanging off my arm? I could hardly wait to see the look on Parker's face.

Just as we were getting out of the taxi, "Someday Soon" started playing. It was Nick.

"Hey Nick, how's Uluru?"

"We didn't make it there. Kitty's birthstone is opal, so she wanted to go to Winton for me to buy her one. So, I rented a plane, and that's where we are."

"Winton, whoa! That's a bit off the beaten track, isn't it?"

"Not really, it's in Central West Queensland, so I suppose it's on the way to Uluru. Anyhow, Ty called me and asked me to come to Sydney to help protect him. I thought I'd better ring you first."

"The guy's a drama queen when it's about him. I don't think there's anything you can do, mate. Just enjoy your holiday with Kitty."

"And Lola."

"Oh, right."

"We were in the bar of the Australian Hotel last night and met a bloke from Sydney. He's an opal dealer and a composer. A good bloke, he's going to write a song for Kitty."

"Cool."

"His name is Rod, and he's got a brother who is an author and has a problem that needs to be solved by a private eye. Do you want me to recommend you?"

"Absolutely, but tell him I don't do divorce spying... and it will have to wait until this case is done. Thanks Tonto."

"No problem Kemosabe, you'll have a lot in common with him. He lived in Manila for ten years or so and owned a third share in Foxy's bar. That was the club Ringo Raye owned, wasn't it?"

"Sure was, he probably knew him," I confirmed.

"Anything new on the case?" he inquired.

"I've got Sherri Sun with me right now on the way to meet Malone and Parker."

"Sherri? Chiang's daughter?"

"Yes."

"The black sheep of the family," he chuckled.

"I'd be more inclined to say she's the white sheep, and the rest of the family are the black ones."

"I hear you. Say hi to her for me. I haven't seen her since she was a kid. I'll call you in a day or two."

"Okay buddy, ciao," I turned to Sherri, who was chilling against the low brick fence out front of Police HQ. "That was Nick Vargas. He asked to say hello to you."

"Oh yeah, the Filipino leg of the family. He's an alright guy."

We went inside to take the elevator up to homicide.

CHAPTER TWENTY-EIGHT

I **WAS RIGHT** about the reaction to Sherri. If Jazz had turned heads, then Sherri just about screwed them off. Through the glass-panelled door, I could see Rick and Parker making notes on the murder board. I knocked on the door and then opened it.

"Rick, got a moment?"

"Come in, mate. Who's this?" he exploded, his eyes bugging out.

Parker turned from the board and reacted in a similar fashion, not at all the same as she had with Jazz. I suppose because Sherri wasn't exuding the arrogance Jazz did.

"This is Sherri Sun, daughter of Chiang Sun, and she's here to help us," I announced.

The discussions went well, and within an hour, we'd hatched a plan to expose the killer. It would require me to stay at Sherri's house in Rockdale. DS Grant Lee would be brought into the case tomorrow under the guise that Rick needed an investigator on board with special knowledge of Triads and fluency in Cantonese. There would be no mention of the death threat against Sun family members. He would be told I'm no longer on the case, and that it's now a police investigation into the murders of Chiang Sun and Rosy Tong. The trap was set, now all we needed was for Grant Lee to spring it.

I phoned Ty and Jazz, told them the plan, and they bought into it. By sundown, after picking up a few things from my apartment, Sherri and I were in a taxi on our way to her home on Kent Street in Rockdale.

~ ~ ~

It was a cul-de-sac with her house right at the end, an old Federation red brick house that, from the outside, didn't seem to match her style at all. The taxi pulled up in the driveway, and we got out.

"I only rent this place, but it suits me fine. I live alone and can walk to work from here. Everything I need is nearby," she said, leading me up the fifteen red stairs to the front door.

"Got a car?" I said, looking at the red roller door on the garage.

"Don't need one."

We went inside.

"There are three bedrooms. Mine is the main one. Take your pick from the other two."

"What's at the back?"

"A small backyard."

"Show me," I said, needing to get a grasp of the entire layout.

"Oh, I forgot. You've got to do the James Bond thing and check the house out for when the crooks arrive," she said, leading me down a hallway to the kitchen and then the back door. I checked the lock and opened a small door off to the right.

"The laundry," she said smugly, with her arms folded.

"Yes, with a window that's open." I locked it. "I'll take the bedroom at the front of the house, so I can keep an eye on things."

"Hey, that's my bedroom," she complained.

"Bad luck," I said with a big Cheshire cat grin.

A couple of hours later, I was sitting on the double bed reading when Sherri called out, "Dinner!" from the dining room. She had put on quite a spread with a number of small dishes in traditional Chinese fashion.

"Seems all I've eaten of late is Chinese food."

"Oh, of course. You've probably been spoiled with all the lovely food from the Golden Dragon."

"Yes, plus I was in Hong Kong with Nick for a few days, and he took me to a couple of his favourite haunts."

"Great. How long have you known Nick?"

"I worked with him on a kidnapping case in Manila a few months back, so not that long. But when you've been put in a life-threatening situation with someone, it's amazing how close you become. It's as though we've been mates for years."

"That makes sense. He's a really rich guy, but he's humble, and that's the sign of a gracious person."

"Yes, he's very generous and caring... that's rare, rich or not."

"You're an oddball, Axis Stone," she said with a smile.

"Yeah, why's that, Sherri Sun?"

"You have a hardball job. You don't need to care about people, but you do. It must be tough being a romantic in your game."

I sat back in my chair and looked her over. "I could say the same of you, couldn't I?"

"No, not at all. My lot in life is to give pleasure, and I pride myself on doing just that."

"Giving pleasure gives you pleasure, huh?"

"Yes, it's a Zen thing."

"Ah, so you're a Buddhist?"

"Sort of... Tantric Buddhism or Vajrayana... the study of Tantric sex."

"Tantric sex? Is that some kind of religion?"

"Tantric texts state that sexual activity can have three separate and distinct purposes: procreation, pleasure, and liberation. Those who use tantric sex to seek liberation abstain from reaching an orgasm in favour of a higher form of ecstasy."

"And what? You practice this and you teach that?"

"Yes."

"Where do I sign up?" I said with a chuckle.

She reached out, took my hand, and gave it a gentle squeeze. "Come."

She walked me into the lounge room. It reminded me of a Hippie flat I'd once been in. I sat on the lounge that was draped with an Indian rug, elephants and tassels on it. She lit a stick of white sage incense, then sat beside me on the lounge and took my hand again. Then we were looking steadily into each other's eyes, and with a quickening of my breath, I knew we were on the brink of something. The air in the room crackled with expectancy. She let go of my hand and rose to her feet.

"Can I get you a drink?" she said, moving over to a small bar.

"Yes, a neat bourbon if you have any."

"I do."

I leaned back on the sofa and watched the dark Chinese dragons in the pattern of her dress appear to move with her. She poured me a drink and brought it back.

"I enjoy being a happy person and making other people happy," she explained, "in terms of being fulfilled."

She was looking into my eyes again, and it seemed the most natural thing in the world to slip my arm around her shoulder and ease her in to snuggle against me. She sighed. "That's nice. You have strong arms, Axis."

"All the better to hold you with, Sherri," I countered.

~ ~ ~

It was in the small hours of the morning that I was suddenly awakened. I had noticed when Sherri led me to bed that the wooden floorboards creaked in certain places in the hallway, and that must have been in the back of my mind because a loud creak woke me. My .38 was in a carry bag beside the bed. I sat up sharply and reached down for it. Sherri was still sound asleep. I got out of bed buck-naked, gun in hand, went to the bedroom door, and slipped silently behind it. The door handle rattled ever so slightly. I held my breath and locked my finger on the trigger of the .38. The hinges squeaked as the door slowly opened. It wasn't too dark—enough of the streetlight from outside streamed in through the bay windows for me to make out a guy dressed in black entering with what looked like a meat cleaver clutched in his hand. Is there only one of them? Should I shoot him or just hold him up? Could I fight him naked? Too many thoughts were spinning through my mind... Instinct was driving me... I lashed out and struck the hand carrying the cleaver hard with my pistol. It hit the floor with a loud clunk and woke Sherri. She sat up, gasped, and turned on the bedside light. He was well in through the door, so I threw a punch at his head. He anticipated it, ducked back, and quickly pulled the door half-closed in one sharp movement. My fist belted into the edge of the door, and the pain shot up my arm like a lightning bolt. It felt like I had broken my wrist. Ignoring the pain, I quickly pulled the door open with my foot, and with the .38 held up to shoot, went after him. I heard movement in the hallway... he was headed for the front door. It was darker there, and with him all in black, he was just a fleeting shadow. I thought of peeling off a blind shot but decided against it. I saw a light; he had opened the front door to slip out. I ran after him outside onto the landing. He was too quick for me to get a bead on him. With the .38 aimed at him, I watched along the sights as he disappeared inside a waiting car. It was already facing out of the cul-de-sac with the engine running, and it shot off. It had no plates. I charged down the stairs, but by the time I got to the bottom, the car was out of sight. The lights came on in the house opposite, and an old lady ripped open the curtains of her front room and gawked at me in wide-eyed terror. I suddenly remembered I was standing stark naked with my .38 in my hand—no wonder she was at the window all goggle-eyed.

CHAPTER TWENTY-NINE

WHEN I TOLD Rick the story over the phone the next
morning, he found the tag most amusing, but he was at
the same time concerned the perps had got away. This
meant a change of plans: the bad guys were now aware Sherri was
under protection. With my apartment the more secure option, it was
a no-brainer for Sherri to stay there, and it didn't take much
convincing. She packed a few things, and we jumped a cab to the
Regal Apartments.

On the way, I phoned Jazz, who wasn't impressed with Sherri
moving in with me. "Next you'll be sleeping together, I know her,
she's a nymphomaniac, won't be able to keep her hands off you," Jazz
exclaimed.

"I wouldn't be too worried about that, Jazz. I can handle it," I
reassured her.

After a brief conversation, Jazz commented, "You're lucky you
didn't get hurt in the attack."

"Yeah, I'm going to the hospital after I drop Sherri off to get my
wrist X-rayed. It's swollen up like a balloon and giving me grief," I
responded.

I got no sympathy from her, something she had in common with
her father. "So, what's Rick's take on the next move?" she asked curtly.

"He and Parker are still mulling it over," I said, not eager to go
into details. In fact, they'd set a meeting with Grant Lee.

"Parker doesn't like me, does she?" Jazz said gruffly.

"I think she might give that impression, but it's just her manner of scrutinising people," I said dismissively, not keen to go there. "I'm going to ring Ty now. Have you spoken to him today?"

"No. Okay, catch you later," Jazz said abruptly, then hung up.

I shrugged my shoulders and dialled Ty's number. After giving him the same story as I had with Jazz, he gave me the same reaction: he didn't care about the details if it involved Sherri but was concerned about the killer targeting him and Jazz.

"Listen, I checked my account and you haven't paid me. Can you fix that up today?" I grated.

"I'll fix it up when I'm convinced there's a plan," he stuttered frantically.

"Ty, you're paying me for work done. I don't go risking my life for nothing. You owe me money, so pay up or you'll find yourself working alone," I asserted.

He got the hint and changed his tone. "All right, Axis, I'm sorry. I'll deposit the money in your account today."

"Okay, I'll ring you back later with the new strategy," I concluded, ending the call. I knew he wasn't going to pay me until he'd heard what he wanted to hear: that the coast was clear.

~ ~ ~

The coffee was brewing while Sherri cleaned up my apartment. There was quite a collection of dirty dishes and clothes to be washed.

I sat on the lounge with my coffee after lacing it with JD. Sherri came up behind me and started massaging my neck, head, and shoulders. That really got the blood flowing to my brain and started me thinking clearer.

"Your wrist looks like it might be fractured," she said.

"Yeah, I'll go to St. Vincent's Hospital and get it X-rayed later this morning. It's bloody sore," I replied.

"They'll only set it and put it in a cast. Do you want me to do it?" she offered.

"Why not? What do you need?" I asked.

"These days you don't really need a plaster cast. We can get a fiberglass brace from a pharmacy," Sherri explained.

"Okay, there's one in Chinatown. I'll go check there," I decided.

"We'll need to get the swelling down first," Sherri advised.

Though my wrist was throbbing, I felt pretty good about myself as I strode along Sussex Street on my way to the Chinatown Pharmacy. The sunny weather lifted my spirits. I was thinking about Nick and the fresh case he had for me. He had sent me the contact for the author who needed a PI. It was good to know I had another job lined up after this one. Ty and Jazz were beginning to get on my nerves, so the sooner this case was over, the better. I had thought about Suzie and decided to give her a quick call in Manila. It came as a surprise when the maid answered and told me Suzie had left. There was a note Dom had photographed and sent to Nick. I hung up and immediately rang Nick, but it went to his voicemail. I left a message, asking him to call me.

~ ~ ~

For some reason, while I was walking, I recalled the nightmare of Rosy with the vampire teeth and wondered why it was still in my mind. I brushed the thought aside and entered the chemist. After ten minutes, I emerged with a carry bag containing a fiberglass wrist brace. The chemist had examined my injury and suggested it might be a slight fracture or a bad strain with deep bruising. He said the brace would do the trick either way. Being Chinese, he recommended using White Flower Oil to hasten healing and reduce pain, so I bought a bottle as well, embracing all things Chinese, both physically and metaphorically.

It was late morning, and I was expecting calls from Rick and Nick, so I swung by the office on the way back to the apartment to check my mail.

Upon reaching my post box, I found it filled with bills, brochures, and pamphlets. Numerous letters of demand from my telco greeted me, and I was surprised my phone hadn't been disconnected.

I discarded most of the junk in the bin and entered the elevator. Just as I stepped out on my floor, "Someday Soon" started playing. It was Nick calling.

"Hey Nick," I greeted him.

"We just got to Uluru," he informed me.

"Good-o, mate. The signal's bad," I noted.

"Yes, you're breaking up as well. Wait, that's better," Nick replied.

I had stopped by the window on the landing. "I won't hold you up. I was just wondering if you got a message from Dom about Suzie?"

"Yes, I was going to send it, we've only just landed," Nick replied.

"What does it say?" I inquired.

"She met a Taiwanese businessman at a shopping mall, and she's gone to stay with him," Nick revealed.

"Oh well, comme ci comme ça — such is life," I said nonchalantly.

"You're in a prophetic mood today, Kemosabe," Nick remarked.

"Yeah, it's either the busted wrist or the wonder of Sherri Sun," I joked.

"Oh no, you haven't, have you?" Nick asked.

"Well, I don't have Suzie anymore... so—" I trailed off.

"You're a rascal, Axis. You can't control yourself; you need to see a therapist," Nick scolded.

"Last time I saw a therapist, she ended up being my girlfriend. No, I'm fine, mate. It's just the way I am," I explained.

"Do you ever not have relations with your clients?" Nick inquired.

"I've had a couple of grannies that I left to nature. Mate, a man has to back himself," I replied confidently.

"You're despicable," Nick teased.

"So, what now? You've gone from Tonto to Daffy Duck? Get out of here," I joked. "Enjoy Uluru, and see if you can pick up a pair of Kurdaitcha shoes for me."

"What are they?" Nick asked curiously.

"Aboriginals reckon when you're wearing them, you're made invisible," I explained.

"Being invisible would only get you into more trouble, my friend. See you, Axis. Be careful," Nick cautioned.

"Likewise, buddy," I said, ending the call.

I opened my office door, entered, flopped into the chair behind my desk, and booted up my computer. Chuckling to myself, I thought, Nick must think I'm a stud — hmm, maybe I am?

I wrote down the name and contact details of the guy Nick recommended for my next case and then attended to paying a bunch of outstanding bills online. At least my credit card was still valid.

The pile of emails in my inbox dated back to before the case began. It was unreasonable and took ages to download all two-thousand, of them. Most were spam, so I swiftly trashed them. However, one email caught my attention. It was from rosyT177. In a delayed reaction, it rang a bell, so I went back to the trash to look for it. To my surprise, it was from Rosy Tong herself. The email said, "Last night was the best ever. Love, Rosy." There was an attachment. When I opened it, I nearly fell out of my chair. She must have emailed me from her iPod only minutes before she was killed. It contained the cryptic message she had mentioned — "I sent you." It was repeated by the vampire version of her in the awful nightmare. She had indeed sent me something. I quickly turned on the printer.

Next, I phoned Rick. He was just about to start the meeting with Parker and Lee. I had to leave a message for him to delay it because I now had critical evidence and was on my way to show him.

~ ~ ~

It didn't take me long to hail a cab outside of the office. I quickly got in and immediately dialled Sherri's number, asking her to meet me right away in front of the apartment block.

We arrived just as Sherri emerged from the front doors.

Ten minutes later, we stepped out of the elevator onto the homicide floor of Police HQ. Sherri wasn't dressed to kill this time, but she still managed to turn a few heads. During the taxi ride, I had briefed her on what would happen in Rick's office.

I knocked on the glass door. "Come in, Axis," Rick called from inside.

We entered and took the chairs that were waiting for us.

"I think you'd better record this, Rick," I advised.

Parker stood up, set up a microphone, and then date and time stamped it on the computer. "Recording," she confirmed.

Lee didn't appear very comfortable with the idea of being recorded, but before he could protest, I said, "Grant Lee, this is Sherri Sun, but then you already know that, don't you?"

With a furrowed brow, he gave Sherri a once-over. "No, I don't think I've ever had the pleasure. Why is this being recorded?"

I ignored his question. "Oh, but you knew her father, Chiang Sun, didn't you?"

"No, only by reputation," he said with a poker face.

I glanced surreptitiously at Rick, and he gave me a nod to continue.

"When did you complete your last undercover assignment, Detective Lee?" I asked sternly.

"August last year. That has nothing to do with this case. Rick, why am I being questioned? Stone isn't a police officer," he complained, starting to look a little unsettled.

"What is your Chinese name?" Parker continued.

"Lee Kit Wo. I still don't see the point of this," he growled intolerantly.

Parker ignored his attitude and asked, "What is your brother's Chinese name?"

"Lee Kok Lung."

Parker took notes while questioning. "Is your brother, Lee Kok Lung, the Hong Kong Dragon Head of the Triad movement Sun Yee On?"

"Yes, but it is a legitimate business," he claimed defensively.

"Do you know Fatty Tung?" I asked.

He jumped up out of his chair and snapped, "I'm not going to be subjected to questions from this man!"

"Sit down, Detective Lee," Rick snarled. "I invited Axis Stone to this meeting to provide evidence in the shark leg case. You will answer his questions."

He slowly sat back down, scowling.

"Do you know Fatty Tung?" I repeated.

"Yes, he works for my brother," he answered indignantly.

"Why was he in Sydney this week?"

"I expect for business," he shrugged his shoulders.

"I put it to you that you are the Dragon Head of the Sydney chapter of Sun Yee On," Parker pressed him.

"That's absurd. In case you haven't noticed, I'm a police officer," he said scornfully.

It was time to use my trump card. I pulled out two sheets of paper from my inside jacket pocket and unfurled them slowly. I watched Lee's beady eyes follow me as I stood and took a couple of steps to hand one to Rick. I turned slowly and handed the other to Lee, then sat back down.

Both men studied the page in their hands. Rick passed his to Parker to check over.

I asked, "Do you recognise the men in that photo, Detective Lee?"

"Yes, Chiang Sun and myself," he said undaunted.

"Do you see the date on the photo, Detective Lee?"

He nodded and looked back at me smugly. His whole demeanour had changed; now he looked to me like a cheap gangster.

"You're on record as saying you never met Chiang Sun, Detective. Your undercover assignment finished in August last year, so what were you doing two months ago handing over drugs to Chiang Sun?" Parker barked.

"I might have been mistaken," he said calmly, nastily.

Sherri eyeballed him with a wicked glint in her eyes. Suddenly, she jumped up and exploded at him, "You killed my father, and you killed Rosy, you bastard! You're a murderer!" Then she launched a second tirade at him in Cantonese. I used to think Cantonese sounded angry in normal conversation, but her attack was so venomous it made normal seem submissive. Sherri had blown her top; she struck out at him with her long fingernails, trying to claw his face off. Parker had to act quickly and only just managed to subdue her before she could do any real damage. Rick nodded sharply toward the door for Parker to take Sherri outside.

Rick announced emphatically, "Lee Kit Wo, I'm charging you with the murders of Chiang Sun and of Rosy Tong. I am also charging you with conspiracy to kidnap Jazz Sun."

With a quick wave of his hand, two uniforms stormed into the office and cuffed Lee.

"Even your lousy photo won't be enough to make any of this stick, Malone. You know that," he sniggered wickedly.

"If the photo isn't so damning, then why did you kill Rosy for it?" I snarled. I wanted to belt his supercilious head in, but I'd have to leave that for his cellmates.

I stood up, eyeballed him, and snarled, "You're just a piece of garbage, Lee, you and your insignificant mob of thugs. This isn't China, and your stand-over tactics don't work here."

"We'll see about that," he cracked back at me through narrowed eyes.

"You've shamed the trust invested in you as a police officer, Lee," Rick growled.

I added, "By the time you get out of prison, you'll be an old man full of regrets. So... we'll see about that!"

"Take him away," Rick roared dismissively.

As they took him out, I noticed Sherri and Parker on their way back to the office. Sherri stopped in her tracks, fired Lee a wicked glare in passing — if looks could kill. Then she shouted something at him in Cantonese.

"Sit down, Axis. A job well done, son," Rick said. "How the hell did you get that photo?"

"Rosy had sent it to my email address before she was killed. I feel like a complete idiot. It had been there all along."

"You weren't meant to know she'd sent it."

"She sent a text with the words 'I sent...' I had no idea what she meant. Today was the first time I've checked my email since I started the case."

"We'll be able to throw the book at him now. The photo should make it stick," Parker said, sitting down.

"Maybe it'll help us crack Fang. He might spill the beans once he knows we've got the Dragon Head," Rick added.

"I think you should have someone interrogate him in Cantonese, Detective," Sherri pointed out.

"I think you might be right. It wouldn't hurt to fly Detective Shun Zhong down from Hong Kong to do it. There's no one savvier on Triads than him," I proposed.

"That's a mighty idea, Axis. I'll do that," Rick said. "So, what's the next case?"

I raised my arm to show the wrist brace. "I've got to mend this first, then I'll see what comes my way." I got up. "Come on, Sherri. Let's go visit your relatives. See you later, Rick. You too, Parker."

~ ~ ~

When we were outside, I called Ty. He was over the moon when I told him the case was solved, and he showered me with praise. It was ironic that Rosy, the girl he had maligned, ended up being his saviour, but I didn't mention it for obvious reasons.

"Have you made the deposit in my account, Ty?" I asked.

"I was onto it when you called, don't worry, you'll be paid in full today," he replied.

I knew he was lying about being onto it, but I was confident he would pay up now that he had received the good news.

"I'll give Jazz a call and tell her. Keep the high security until tomorrow. By then, Rick will have lodged formal charges against Lee, and the threat to both of you will be derailed," I explained.

"Thank you, Axis," Ty expressed his gratitude.

I hung up and then dialled Jazz to deliver the news. She understood the irony and was thankful for Rosy's clever deed.

"Should I dismiss the bodyguard?" she asked.

"No, not until I give you the word. You're not safe until Lee is behind bars," I cautioned.

"Are you thinking there might be more reprisals for my father's actions?" she inquired.

"How long is a piece of string? I can't answer that, honey. Right now, we believe we have the Dragon Head of the Sydney chapter of Sun Yee On, who might have been operating on an agenda of his own... or the whole issue was orchestrated by Lee Kok Lung, the Dragon Head in Hong Kong, and Lee was just a pawn in a much bigger game. The reason why Fatty Tung came here for your handover is still a mystery. Was it just to get even with me?" I pondered.

"I see what you're saying. There could be a bigger picture," Jazz responded with a hint of nervousness.

"We'll only know that when and if Rick and Parker get Lee to talk," I said.

"And what are the chances of that happening?" she asked.

"Rick is going to fly Detective Shun Zhong, the boss of the Organised Crime and Triad Bureau in Hong Kong, to Sydney to interrogate him in Cantonese. If anyone can do it, I'd bet on him," I explained.

"That's an excellent idea. Look, how about coming over for dinner tonight, leg man? I promise a sensuous barefoot dessert," Jazz offered.

"Sorry, Jazz. I'll have to take a raincheck. I've got a busted wrist," I declined.

"Sherri is your nurse now?" she teased.

"Let's just say she's got the healing touch. Oh, by the way, do you need me to text you my account details?" I asked.

"Yes, do that, Axis," she replied in a churlish tone. "Call me tomorrow." She hung up abruptly, clearly displeased that she had been replaced.

Well, you win some and you lose some when it comes to dames. Some are missing that one special ingredient that presses the right buttons for me. Sherri has it, and Jazz doesn't. I suppose Suzie had it too, and Rosy certainly did. It makes me wonder if it's a certain vulnerability that attracts me, or is it something deeper that I sense in some women? It's probably a combination of factors. Maybe it's the difference between wanting me for their own pleasure and wanting to share a special moment of intimate ecstasy with me—the operative word being "share." But then again I really can't claim to be the best judge of the female species—if I was I'd write the book and make millions.

The case was pretty much done and dusted. I could do no more. It was now a matter of being a creature of habit and changing my ringtone.

"What are you doing?" Sherri asked.

"I'm changing my ringtone from "Someday Soon" back to another one of my favourites, "The Terrible Tango.""

"Why? What a funny name," she commented.

"I use a different ringtone for each case. Just a quirky habit," I explained.

"But you don't have a new case yet," she pointed out.

"Oh, something will pop up soon enough. It always does," I assured her.

"In the meantime, do you want me to stay with you, or should I go back home?" she asked.

I instructed the cabby to let us out at the corner of Goulburn Street.

I checked my bank account at the ATM, and both Ty and Jazz had paid up. It was the healthiest my account had ever looked. That called for celebration, so I bought a vintage bottle of JD No. 27 Gold Tennessee Whiskey from a nearby liquor store. Normally, I wouldn't spend that much money on booze, but hell, this was a special occasion, and besides, it was guaranteed to dull the pain in my wrist.

As my old dad used to say about whiskey, "A little medicine goes a long way."

~ ~ ~

The next morning, there wasn't a drop left of the JD No. 27 when I tried to pour it into my coffee—we'd certainly given it a nudge. My wrist-brace had me making a mockery of the effort to put two slices of bread into the toaster. Sherri was still asleep, and I heard a muffled version of "The Terrible Tango" ring out. I rummaged through the pile of clothes on the living room floor and found the phone just before it went to voicemail. It was Rick calling. He and Parker had been up all night interrogating Grant Lee and had eventually extracted a confession: he is the Dragon Head of the Sydney chapter of Sun Yee On. To put my mind at ease, they had determined that Fatty Tung had come to Sydney of his own accord to get square with me for nailing his mate Soy Ling Chu. They had taken my recommendation, and Zhong would be arriving today to assist with the final interrogation of both Lee Kit Wo and Fang Peng Jian.

It seemed my concern that our celebration last night might have been premature was completely unfounded because, as far as I was concerned, the case was closed. I called Ty and Jazz to share the good news.

The End

Don't miss the next adventure in Book 3:

SMUGGLER'S HOLE